Performance Measurement Systems in Banks

Given the significant changes in the banking environment and the resultant pressures on banks to change their systems and procedures, this book is a timely reference that provides a comprehensive analytical overview of changes in the performance measurement system (PMS) of banks in the post-financial crisis era. It explores the factors that influence such changes and examines banks' consequential responses to institutional pressures. It is an invaluable resource for researchers and practitioners to gain insights into the concept of PMS change in both developed and developing economies.

Rahat Munir is Professor and Head of Department in the Department of Accounting and Corporate Governance at Macquarie University, Australia.

Kevin Baird is Professor in Accounting at the Department of Accounting and Corporate Governance of Macquarie University, Australia.

T0371721

Routledge International Studies in Money and Banking

For more information about this series, please visit www.routledge.com/series/
SE0403

Performance Measurement Systems in Banks

Rahat Munir and Kevin Baird

Routledge
Taylor & Francis Group

LONDON AND NEW YORK

First published 2019
by Routledge
2 Park Square, Milton Park, Abingdon, Oxon OX14 4RN

and by Routledge
605 Third Avenue, New York, NY 10017

First issued in paperback 2020

Routledge is an imprint of the Taylor & Francis Group, an informa business

British Library Cataloguing-in-Publication Data
A catalogue record for this book is available from the British Library

Library of Congress Cataloging-in-Publication Data
Names: Munir, Rahat, author | Baird, Kevin, author.
Title: Performance measurement systems in banks / by Rahat Munir
  and Kevin Baird.
Description: Abingdon, Oxon ; New York, NY : Routledge, 2019. |
  Series: Routledge international studies in money and banking ; 99 |
  Includes bibliographical references and index.
Identifiers: LCCN 2018038041 | ISBN 9781138556713 (hardback) |
  ISBN 9781315150277 (ebook)
Subjects: LCSH: Bank management. | Banks and banking. |
  Performance—Measurement.
Classification: LCC HG1615 .M86 2019 | DDC 332.1068—dc23
LC record available at https://lccn.loc.gov/2018038041

ISBN 13: 978-0-367-50432-8 (pbk)
ISBN 13: 978-1-138-55671-3 (hbk)

Typeset in Galliard
by Apex CoVantage, LLC

Contents

Figures

Tables

Acknowledgements

I would like to acknowledge all the support I received from academic and administrative staff from both the Department of Accounting and Corporate Governance, and the Faculty of Business and Economics, Macquarie University. Many thanks are also due to those respondents from the case organisation in Pakistan who took the time to respond to the questionnaire, participated in the interviews, and provided relevant documents. I would also like to express my sincere gratitude to the participants of the research, including the Executives of FUB and State Bank of Pakistan for providing documents concerning the banking sector in Pakistan.

Finally, I am thankful and indebted to my family (my wife Meena and children Danyal, Talha, Shahrukh, and Laiba) and parents for their continuous support and encouragement throughout this book.

Abbreviations

AICPA	American Institute of Certified Public Accountants
ATM	Auto Teller Machine
BIS	Bank for International Settlements
BSC	Balanced Scorecard
CAELS	Capital adequacy, Assets quality, Earning quality, Liquidity, and Sensitivity
CAMELS	Capital adequacy, Assets quality, Management, Earning quality, Liquidity, and Sensitivity
CRWA	Capital to Risk-Weighted Assets Ratio
FASB	Financial Accounting Standard Board
GDP	Gross Domestic Product
HSBC	Hong Kong and Shanghai Banking Corporation
IASB	International Accounting Standard Board
IFAC	International Federation of Accountants
IFRS	International Financial Reporting Standard
IMF	International Monetary Fund
ISA	International Statements of Auditing
ISO	International Organization for Standardization
KFW Development Bank	Kreditanstalt Für Wiederaufbau – German Development Bank
KPI	Key Performance Indicator
NCCC	National Credit Consultative Council
NIS	New Institutional Sociology
OAEM	other assets especially mentioned
OECD	Organisation for Economic Co-operation and Development
PBC	Pakistan Banking Council
PMS	Performance Measurement System
ROI	Return on Investment
RSA	Rate Sensitive Assets
RSL	Rate Sensitive Liabilities
SBP	State Bank of Pakistan
UNO	United Nations Organization
WHO	World Health Organization
WTO	World Trade Organization

1 Introduction

1.1 Background

Performance measurement systems (PMS), as a fundamental element of management control, are used for the efficient and effective management of organisations (Langfield-Smith et al., 2009). These systems are mainly designed to provide useful information to support strategic decision making, planning, and the control of activities in order to accomplish organisational goals (Merchant and Van der Stede, 2007; Neely et al., 2002; Kaplan and Norton, 1996). Traditionally these systems have been dominated by financial measures, such as Earnings per Share, Return on Investment, and Return on Equity. The aim of such systems was to ensure that, from a shareholders' point of view, the organisation's performance was financially successful and that progress was in accordance with the business plan (Bititci et al., 2000; Neely, 1998; Dixon et al., 1990). While such traditional PMSs were developed in the early 20th century, their usefulness has become limited over the years due to the rapid change in the organisational environment. For instance, Burns and Scapens (2000) state that:

> The environment in which management accounting is practised certainly appears to have changed, with advances in information technology, more competitive markets, different organizational structures, and new management practices.
>
> (p. 3)

The complexity and scope of change[1] in the organisational environment has led management accounting researchers (e.g., Kennerley and Neely, 2003; Norreklit, 2000; Neely, 1999; Otley, 1999; Ittner and Larcker, 1998; Atkinson et al., 1997; Johnson and Kaplan, 1987) to criticise traditional PMSs[2] for their excessive reliance on financial performance measures. Johnson and Kaplan (1987), in this context, claim that financial information used for measurement purposes has been too late, too aggregated, and too distorted to be relevant to managers' planning and control decisions. Consequently, there have been various attempts to develop systems that overcome the limitations of traditional financial-based PMSs with new (or contemporary) PMSs including the Performance Measurement Matrix (Keegan et al.,

1989), the performance (SMART) Pyramid (Lynch and Cross, 1991), the Results and Determinants Framework (Fitzgerald et al., 1991), the Balanced Scorecard (Kaplan and Norton, 1992), the Performance Prism (Neely and Adams, 2001), and the Comparative Business Scorecard (Kanji and Moura, 2002). A detailed review of these contemporary PMSs is provided in Chapter 2 of this book.

In contrast to traditional PMSs, the focus of contemporary PMSs is on multidimensional perspectives of organisational performance, utilising both financial and non-financial measures as well as leading and lagging indicators, linking performance measures to the vision, goals, and strategy of the organisation, and providing a way to translate organisational strategy into a coherent set of performance measures (Anthony and Govindarajan, 2007; Lord, 2007; Chenhall, 2005; Neely et al., 2001; Kaplan and Norton, 1992, 1996).

Evidence suggests that organisations are moving towards these contemporary PMSs with fifty per cent of the organisations in North America and forty per cent in Europe having significantly changed their measurement practices by the end of the 1990s (Frigo and Krumwiede, 1999). In Australia, McCunn (1998) found that thirty per cent of the top 1,000 organisations were adopting contemporary PMSs. However, despite the perceived benefits of contemporary PMSs, some studies have found that contemporary PMSs, such as the Balanced Scorecard, are not widely used. For instance, in public sector organisations, Perera et al. (2007) revealed that only seventeen per cent of the respondents from Sydney local councils had adopted the Balanced Scorecard or were in the process of adopting it. In a similar vein, Chan (2004) examined the adoption of the Balanced Scorecard in North America, and found that only eight per cent and six per cent of municipal governments in the United States and Canada respectively had adopted the Balanced Scorecard.

These conflicting findings raise the fundamental question as to why some organisations have changed their PMSs while others have refrained from doing so. More specifically, what factors influence some organisations to change their PMSs and what factors prevent others from introducing such change? In addressing this question, numerous authors (e.g., Almqvist and Skoog, 2006; Burns and Vaivio, 2001; Greenwood and Hinings, 1996) argue that organisations worldwide are experiencing significant changes in their organisational environments, largely driven by globalisation, increased competition, and advancements in information technologies. These changes have generated pressures for organisations to adapt their systems and procedures (Chow and Van der Stede, 2006; Bourne et al., 2000; Waggoner et al., 1999; Kaplan and Norton, 1992; Johnson and Kaplan, 1987) with many organisations implementing new technologies and management practices (Neely et al., 1994; Banker et al., 1993). Hence, the adoption of new technologies and management practices has forced organisations to reconsider the suitability of their PMS, with some organisations making the necessary changes to make the PMS more effective in meeting the challenges of the changing business environment.

However, making changes to PMSs is often problematic due to the lack of adequate and necessary management skills, the lack of support and commitment from employees, and drawbacks in the technologies and processes used to implement new PMSs (Neely et al., 2001; Sinclair and Zairi, 2000; Neely, 1998). In fact, management often becomes frustrated with the technical barriers they face when introducing changes to PMSs and are required to make detailed adjustments which add an additional burden to accommodate such changes (Hoque and James, 2000; Vaivio, 1999; Ittner and Larcker, 1998; Kaplan, 1984). Consequently, some organisations have responded to the pressures emanating from the changes in their organisational environment by maintaining the status quo.

Understanding changes in the organisational environment and the resultant pressures to change PMSs is crucial given the type and magnitude of changes to PMSs will depend on the nature and degree of the changed environmental conditions (Johnson and Kaplan, 1987). Due to this complex relationship between the organisations and their environment, organisations are forced to develop, implement, and use new PMSs. Hence, to introduce changes in PMSs, it is important to understand the factors that influence changes in PMSs, the forms of pressure that enact change, and the ways in which organisations respond to such change efforts. Despite the increasing awareness of the influence of environmental changes and ensuing pressures on PMSs (e.g., Hussain and Hoque, 2002; Ang and Cummings, 1997; Greenwood and Hinings, 1996), the studies undertaken to examine changes in PMSs have often focused on the manufacturing industry with limited studies conducted in relation to PMS change within the banking industry.

The banking industry has experienced major changes in recent times due to the impact of deregulation, advances in information systems and technologies, globalisation, and more recently the global financial crisis triggered by the subprime turmoil in the United States (Wignall and Atkinson, 2010; Lapavitsas and Santos, 2008; Kahveci and Sayilgan, 2006; World Bank, 2005). The speed and intensity with which the banking industry has changed in recent years has led to phenomenal growth in international transactions, the expansion of banking operations across borders, and the restructuring and consolidation of banks. This growth has in turn prompted banks to seek new sources of income, use complex tools for risk assessment and mitigation, and develop greater awareness of their costs and the productivity gains to be realised from work reorganisation and financial innovations (PriceWaterhouseCoopers, 2009; Bank for International Settlements, 2006, 2010; Helliar et al., 2002). Accordingly, in addition to traditional banking products, banks have become more involved in volatile investment activities and financial instruments such as commercial papers, junk bonds, leveraged buyouts, mutual funds, assets securitisation, and derivatives (World Bank, 2008; Citigroup Inc., 2000; Frei et al., 1998).

Additionally, banks have increasingly become subject to immense pressure from their stakeholders to improve performance, forcing them to re-examine their traditional management control approaches and banking technologies, strengthen their capital base, reduce their non-performing and toxic assets, bring down operational costs, enhance corporate governance, and sharpen their customer centric initiatives (Lapavitsas and Santos, 2008; Helliar et al., 2002; Frei et al., 1998). Furthermore, the recent financial crisis which began in mid-2007 has forced banking institutions worldwide to grapple with reduced public confidence, heightened shareholder scrutiny, and increased regulatory insight (Wignall and Atkinson, 2010). Further, the introduction of risk-adjusted performance measurement guidelines by the Bank for International Settlements, the operation of the Basel Accords,[3] and the stringent supervisory control frameworks, such as CAMELS[4] and CAELS,[5] which have been adopted by central banks across the world, have resulted in the significant transformation of banks in respect to organisational structures, systems, and strategies (Geyfman, 2005; World Bank, 2005).

In an attempt to sustain such changes, many banks have adopted technologically sound and sophisticated management practices (Bank of England, 2003). This has led to concerns regarding the suitability of their existing control systems, including PMSs, as it became evident that in order to meet the pressures of the changing organisational environment, management control systems, within which the PMS is a part, should be adjusted before they lose their relevance (Ferreira and Otley, 2009; Modell, 2007; Ittner and Larcker, 1998; Eccles, 1991; Kaplan, 1984). In particular, there has been an increasing need to introduce changes to PMSs in order to develop and adopt innovative and robust solutions for management controls, new databases, and new analytical ways to prudently assess costs, benefits, and risks (PriceWaterhouseCoopers, 2009; Guerreiro et al., 2006; Hawkins and Mihaljek, 2001; Karr, 1997). Hence, it is important that PMSs adapt to the recent environmental conditions as reflected in the following comment by Dixon et al. (1990, pp. 4–5):

> A good measurement system needs to be continually changed in order to remain effective. As one set of goals or objectives is satisfied, or as the set of measures becomes too gross to detect improvement, a new set needs to be articulated, and the old set needs to be discarded or modified. This means there can never be a set of good performance measures that is stable over time.

Accordingly, given the significant changes in the banking environment and the resultant pressures on banks to change their systems and procedures, the motivation of this research is to gain an understanding of PMS change within a bank by examining the factors that influence such change. In this rapidly changing environment an understanding of the factors that influence banks to change their PMSs and the responses of managers to such pressures is vital for researchers and practitioners to gain insights into the concept of PMS change. Banking practitioners will benefit from a better understanding of the factors that influence changes in PMSs, for instance, by making them aware of the need to adapt their structure, strategy, and PMS in order to operate more efficiently and effectively. Banking practitioners who are experiencing pressures due to the change in their wider macro-level and institutional environments could learn from the findings of this research and make adaptations in an attempt to operate on a more commercial and competitive basis. While it is acknowledged that the ability of banks to make PMS change is dependent on the nature of their organisational environment, it is hoped that by highlighting the factors that influence PMS change and the responses to such influencing factors, bank managers will be more aware of the importance of competing on a commercial basis and keeping their PMS up to date.

1.2 Association between PMS of banks and factors influencing them

A review of current literature suggests that although a considerable amount of research addresses issues concerning changes in management accounting systems such as PMSs, the empirical evidence has almost totally been based on data from manufacturing organisations with limited studies examining such issues in the context of banks (e.g., Guerreiro et al., 2006; Soin et al., 2002; Helliar et al., 2002; Ang and Cummings, 1997; Cobb et al., 1995). However, the review of the literature suggests that the management and operational specificities of banks are different from manufacturing organisations. These differences are apparent in the type of products and processes, technology choices, competition, and nature of customers and markets (Drucker, 2003).

While there is a strand of research in management accounting that addresses performance measurement issues within banks (e.g., Helliar et al., 2002; Soin et al., 2002; Hussain and Hoque, 2002; Frei et al., 1998; Cobb et al., 1995), these studies primarily focus on their impact on (i) organisational performance or (ii) the design or development, implementation, and use of PMSs. These studies do not explicitly examine how changes in the wider macro-level environment and ensuing pressures emanating from the changes in the institutional environment, simultaneously or independently, influence PMSs and how banks respond to such pressures, thereby leaving an empirical gap in the field of performance measurement. Such an understanding is crucial for banks as their control systems, including performance measurement practices, are highly vulnerable to the changes in their external environment, such as technological innovations, competition, and regulatory pressures (PriceWaterhouseCoopers, 2011). Hence, the first motivation of this research is to address this void in the management accounting literature.

Similar to developed countries, banks operating in emerging economies have also experienced significant changes in their functioning in recent times due to the impact of deregulation, advances in information systems and technologies, and globalisation (Cull and Peria, 2007; Kahveci and Sayilgan, 2006; World Bank, 2005; Iimi, 2004). In addition to the increasing need to improve efficiency and effectiveness to successfully compete in the contemporary environment, the adoption of new technologies and management practices has forced banks to assess the suitability of their control systems, including PMSs, and to introduce necessary changes to make those systems more effective.[6] Whilst there have been empirical investigations that help to understand the factors that influence banks operating in developed countries to change their PMSs (e.g., Sartorius et al., 2006; Helliar et al., 2002; Hussain and Hoque, 2002; Cobb et al., 1995), this research is motivated by the lack of previous research in the context of banks operating in emerging economies. Many authors (e.g., Cull and Peria, 2007; De Waal, 2007; Chow et al., 1999; Wallace, 1990) have cautioned against the transferability of the findings of studies across economies and have advocated conducting research into understanding changes in management accounting systems, such as the PMS, in an emerging economy context. Similarly, Hawkins and Mihaljek (2001) and Bromwich and Bhimani (1989) argue that the transfer of the results of studies undertaken in developed and foreign surroundings is not reasonable due to the divergent conditions under which different organisations operate. They further argue that consideration should always be made of the political, economic, social, and cultural environments that surround an organisation. For instance, in emerging economies banks are expected to pursue objectives (other than profit maximisation alone) such as nationwide financial provision and politically motivated credit allocation to priority sectors (Iimi, 2004, p. 508).

Further, in comparison with emerging economies, banks in developed countries are more independent, with virtually no unsolicited government interference (Bernanke, 2011; Hawkins and Mihaljek, 2001). The Bank for International Settlements (2003) noted that in emerging economies the central banks often compromise on implementing stringent banking regulations to facilitate their governments in achieving fiscal and structural targets. In these economies, fiscal targets are frequently associated with economic disturbances. Such disturbances are rare in developed countries, which are generally less vulnerable to real or financial shocks, and whose governments are less susceptible to financing constraints (Moreno, 2003). Such contextual differences could have implications for control systems, including the PMS they adopt. While there have been some PMS studies on banks (e.g., Guerreiro et al., 2006; Soin et al., 2002; Helliar et al., 2002; Hussain and Hoque, 2002; Soin, 1996; Cobb et al., 1995), with a few exceptions (e.g., Guerreiro et al., 2006), the focus of these studies generally has been on banks operating in developed countries with limited research examining the PMSs of banks operating in emerging economies. It is important that researchers focus on emerging economies as research settings given emerging economies face unique environments which have not been analysed in previous studies (Cull and Peria, 2007; De Waal, 2007; Uddin and Tsamenyi, 2005). Hence, the second motivation of this research is to provide an insight into the factors that influence PMS change in a bank in an emerging economy.

This research also responds to calls from researchers (e.g., Kasurinen, 2002; Burns and Scapens, 2000; Greenwood and Hinings, 1996) to use coherent analytical frameworks in order to understand changes in management accounting systems. In an attempt to assist in understanding changes in management accounting systems, a number of frameworks have been proposed in the literature (e.g., Kasurinen, 2002; Burns and Scapens, 2000; Waggoner et al., 1999; Greenwood and Hinings, 1996; Cobb et al., 1995; Innes and Mitchell, 1990). These frameworks mainly focus on examining the preconditions of change, the process of change, and the consequences of change (Andon et al., 2007). Kasur-inen (2002) and Burns and Scapens (2000) state that many of the frameworks are fragmented and have failed to provide a holistic analysis of the macro-level context of an organisation as well as its institutional context. Further, the responses of management to the factors that influence change have generally not been addressed in these frameworks. Both of these aspects are critically important for analysing changes in management accounting systems (Greenwood and Hinings, 1996). Moreover, according to Cobb et al. (1995), most of these frameworks have been developed in a manufacturing context, and hence their applicability to banking institutions is limited due to the different nature of their business operations and processes, the risks they face, and the nature of their technologies. Consequently, the third motivation of this research is to develop an analytical framework by drawing on multiple theoretical constructs to analyse the factors that influence changes in PMSs within banks and the potential responses or reaction to such influencing factors.

The next chapter of this book provides a broad overview of PMSs. Its main aim is to review the literature outlining the concept of performance measurement within organisations, and to describe the different frameworks used to examine how and why PMSs have changed within organisations. The chapter also describes how the banking industry has changed over the last few decades and the pressures that have emanated from those changes which have consequently forced banks to change their systems and procedures including internal controls and PMSs.

Chapter 3 presents the analytical framework of the research. The chapter begins by describing the wider macro-level factors that affect the functioning of banks and explores how these factors contribute in creating pressures to change PMSs. Subsequently, the theoretical concepts of DiMaggio and Powell's (1983) notion of institutional isomorphism and Oliver's (1991) continuum of strategic responses to institutional pressures are discussed to set the foundation for developing the analytical framework of this research. This chapter concludes with a presentation of the analytical framework that is subsequently used to analyse and examine the empirical data in order to explore the changes in the PMS of the bank investigated.

Chapter 4 describes the research method utilised to collect empirical data. The chapter begins with an overview of the case research approach, its use, limitations, and contribution to management accounting research. This is followed by a detailed discussion of the research site selected for this research and procedures for selection of participants. The chapter continues with a description of the stages of construction of the interview guide and questionnaire, features of the cover letter, and the final content of the interview guide and questionnaire. It also describes the internal and external documents used in this research and concludes with an outline of the method that is used to analyse the data.

Chapters 5 and 6 contain the findings of the research. Chapter 5 provides the background of the bank's external environment prior to 1997, the year in which financial sector reforms were initiated in Pakistan. This chapter illustrates the nature of the reforms and their impact on the banking sector as a whole. It also describes the economic, technological, political, and social context of Pakistan just prior to 1997. Chapter 6 provides a detailed analysis of the PMS changes that took place in the case organisation during 1997–2007 and beyond, and the responses to the pressures the case organisation faced to change its PMS.

Chapter 7 provides the conclusions of the research. It also provides an overview of the research's theoretical and empirical contributions to the performance measurement literature. Additionally, the chapter presents a brief account of the limitations and the possibilities for further research.

Notes

1 The research on organisational change regards change as a continuous, unpredictable process driven by environmental instability that organisations try to overcome through different modifications and adaptations (Burns and Vaivio, 2001).
2 The terms 'traditional PMSs' and 'conventional PMSs' have the same meaning. Hence, they are used interchangeably in many places in the management accounting literature.
3 Basel Accords are the frameworks released by the Basel Committee on banking supervision of the Bank for International Settlements (BIS). Basel Accord I was released in 1988 which was later replaced with Basel Accord II in 2004. The Basel Accord II rested on three pillars: minimum capital requirements (pillar 1), guidelines on regulatory intervention to national supervisors (pillar 2), and new information disclosure standards for banks (pillar 3). In a response to the global financial crisis the Basel Committee has drafted Basel Accord III to replace Basel Accord II from 2012.
4 The CAMELS framework involves analysis of specific groups of performance measures namely Capital adequacy, Assets quality, Management, Earning quality, Liquidity, and Sensitivity (market risk).
5 The CAELS framework involves analysis of five groups of performance measures namely Capital adequacy, Assets quality, Earning quality, Liquidity, and Sensitivity to other risks.
6 Efficiency is generally concerned with achieving given results with minimum resources and effectiveness while attaining organisational objectives (Anthony, 1965).

2 Literature review

2.1 Introduction

The purpose of this chapter is to provide a review of the literature pertinent to the topic of the research with the aim of locating the research within the extant literature. Firstly, the chapter provides a broad overview of literature on the nature of performance measurement systems (PMSs), their purposes, and use within organisations. The chapter also reviews relevant literature that explores and examines how and why PMSs change within organisations. In particular, based on this literature the chapter describes why organisations have become increasingly interested in changing their PMSs, the factors that have influenced them to do so, and their responses to pressures for change. Secondly, the chapter reviews literature on changes in the banking industry over the last few decades and the pressures placed on banks to change their systems and procedures, including internal controls such as PMSs. The review of the literature on the factors that could influence banks to change their PMSs and the banks' responses to change will be used to develop the analytical framework (in Chapter 3) used to examine PMS change in the bank investigated.

2.2 Performance measurement systems in organisations

The PMS is an important subsystem within the control systems of organisations (Zimmerman, 2009; Merchant and Van der Stede, 2007; Chia, 1995; Flamholtz, 1983). Merchant (1998) indicates that management control systems, including PMSs, are devices that managers use to ensure that their actions and decisions are consistent with overall organisational objectives and strategies. According to Anthony and Govindarajan (2007), management control is the process by which managers ensure that resources are obtained and used effectively and efficiently to accomplish an organisation's objectives. Similarly, Drury (2002) states that one of the main purposes of the management control system is to provide information that is useful for measuring performance.[1] Anthony et al. (2011) also note that a management control system consists of a collection of control mechanisms which have traditionally revolved around measuring and controlling organisational activities. Thus, performance measurement is central to management control within any organisation (Merchant and Van der Stede, 2007; Olson and Slater, 2002), and given its significance, this research focuses on PMSs.

The term PMS has been described in the literature in multiple ways. For instance, Marshall et al. (1999) describe a PMS as a development of indicators and a collection of data to describe, analyse, and report organisational performance to management. Neely et al. (1995) consider that performance measurement is vital for measuring the efficiency and effectiveness of actions. They refer to two aspects of a PMS: (i) the set of metrics[2] used to quantify both the efficiency and effectiveness of actions; and (ii) the process of quantifying the efficiency and effectiveness of actions. In a similar vein, Kaplan and Norton (1996) regard a PMS as a system that aims to provide financial and non-financial signals in order to help management make decisions. More recently, Radnor and Lovell (2003) depict the PMS as the means of gathering data to support and coordinate the process of making decisions and taking action throughout the organisation.

Expanding on this definition, Amaratunga and Baldry (2003, p. 174) defined a PMS as:

> A process of assessing the progress towards achieving pre-determined goals, including information on the efficiency with which resources are transformed into goods and services, the quality of those outputs and outcomes, and the effectiveness of organizational operations in terms of their specific contributions to organizational objectives.

These definitions have been criticised for excluding the infrastructure that supports performance measurement, which is an important part of an effective PMS (Bourne et al., 2003; Lowe and Puxty, 1989; Emmanuel et al., 1990; Otley et al., 1995). Therefore, in this research, based on Otley and Berry's (1994) definition, a PMS is defined as the set of procedures, processes, and metrics that organisational participants use for the efficient and effective accomplishment of their goals and the goals of their organisations.

The definitions presented above have described the PMS using different perspectives. For instance, Neely et al. (1995) defined the PMS from an operations perspective. Kaplan and Norton (1996) and Radnor and Lovell (2003) defined the PMS based on its role in management. Otley and Berry (1994) and Marshall et al. (1999) use a definition based on the procedures and processes that are part of the PMS. A review of these definitions also suggests that the nature of a PMS differs from one industrial sector to another and even from one organisation to another. According to Anthony et al. (2011) these differences could depend on the organisational context which could be characterised by complexity and diversity of operations. For instance, some organisations use PMSs only as a reporting mechanism (e.g., management accounting reports) while other organisations utilise PMSs for controlling the performance of products, employees, and processes (e.g., costing systems, staff appraisal and reward systems).

The next two subsections review the literature on PMSs (both traditional[3] and contemporary PMSs) with the intention to explain the nature of these systems, the need to change them, and the changes that took place in these systems over the past couple of decades.

2.2.1 Traditional performance measurement systems and their shortcomings

A review of the management accounting literature indicates the concept of a PMS was formally introduced in the early 1900s when the Du-Pont Company devised financial measures, including Return on Investment, Return on Equity, and Earnings per Share, as performance indicators to evaluate the efficiency of their business processes (Kaplan, 1984). Since then, financial measures have been widely used for measuring performance in most organisations (Johnson and Kaplan, 1987). The aim of traditional PMSs was to ensure that, from a shareholder's viewpoint, the organisation's performance was financially successful and that progress was in accordance with the business plan (Bititci et al., 2002; Neely, 1998; Dixon et al., 1990).

While most of the traditional PMSs were developed in the early 20th century, due to their inherent limitations (e.g., only financial measures, historical data, summary information, lag indicators) their usefulness diminished as the business environment changed in the latter part of the 20th century. Kennerley and Neely (2002), for example, indicate that the mid-1980s saw remarkable changes in PMSs, driven mainly by the development of new technologies, the increasing complexity of organisational operations, and the expansion in markets. The changes in the organisational environment altered the requirements for performance measurement within organisations as management required more focused information on business processes, customers' orientation, continuous improvements, and employee knowledge (Chenhall, 2005; Bourne et al., 2003). It was argued that the traditional PMSs were not capable of meeting these emerging challenges in the organisational environment. For example, Johnson and Kaplan (1987) claimed that:

> In this time of rapid technological change, vigorous global and domestic competition, and enormously expanding information processing capabilities, management accounting systems are not providing useful, timely information for the process control, product costing, and performance evaluation activities of managers.
>
> (Preface: xi)

In particular, Johnson and Kaplan (1987) voiced their dissatisfaction with the high focus on financial measures in traditional PMSs, and emphasised the need for changes in such systems as the information from these systems was not considered appropriate for planning and control. A major criticism of traditional PMSs was that by focusing on short-term objectives, they are not providing an adequate indication of performance for organisations (Langfield-Smith et al., 2009) and disregarding longer-term performance measures such as quality, innovativeness, and customer satisfaction (Bourne et al., 2003; Ghalayini and Noble, 1996; Eccles, 1991). Traditional PMSs have also been criticised for using historical accounting information and failing to focus on the future (Lord, 2007; Pun and White, 2005; Kaplan and Norton, 1996; Neely et al., 1995). These systems also lack alignment with the core organisational objectives that are crucial in ensuring the successful implementation and execution of strategies identified by the organisation (e.g., Lord, 2007; Radnor and Lovell, 2003; Kaplan and Norton, 1992; Eccles, 1991; Maskell, 1989).

Ittner and Larcker (1998) note that the validity and survival of today's organisations are significantly influenced by the strategies they adopt. These strategies and competitive realities require new measurement systems because traditional PMSs that stress financial measures can no longer satisfy the needs of contemporary business organisations (Eccles, 1991). In particular, according to Eccles (1991), globalisation, increasing competition, increased public sophistication, and active consumerism have all contributed to shifting the manifest of PMSs towards the use of non-financial measures such as customer satisfaction and service quality. Non-financial performance measures are regarded as powerful tools that have a capacity to "transform the role of management accounting. Non-financial measures provide more penetrating control, going beyond the limits of aggregated financial measures" (Vaivio, 1999, p. 410). Kaplan and Norton (2001) and Neely et al. (2001) indicate that to be successful and competitive, organisations require a more systematic and thorough approach in measuring their performance by using multidimensional perspectives.

According to Ghalayini and Noble (1996), the challenge which organisations face is to develop PMSs that capture multidimensional aspects of their businesses and measure performance with a strategic focus. In particular, to meet external stakeholders' expectations, organisations need to define their strategies and goals using both financial measures and non-financial measures (Bourne et al., 2003). Hence, financial measures alone cannot provide a clear indication of performance in the critical areas of business operations (Ittner and Larcker, 1998; Kaplan and Norton, 1992) and it is imperative that organisations develop PMSs carefully and choose measures that are derived from strategy and cover different performance perspectives (Chenhall, 2005; Neely et al., 1995; Eccles, 1991). Well-developed PMSs provide management with a sense of knowing what needs to be done without necessarily understanding the intricacies of related processes (Bititci et al., 2000). Poorly developed and outdated or obsolete PMSs can lead to frustration, conflict, and confusion within organisations (Neely, 1998; Atkinson et al., 1997; Kaplan, 1984). Accordingly, PMSs need to be reviewed, updated and/or changed as the needs and expectations of the organisation change to ensure that they provide the desired business results and outcomes (Eccles, 1998). The management accounting literature generally advocates the use of more contemporary PMSs (Modell, 2007; Almqvist and Skoog, 2006; Bourne et al., 2000) with the next subsection providing an overview of these approaches (hereafter called "contemporary PMSs").

2.2.2 Contemporary performance measurement systems

The key features of contemporary PMSs are that they: are multidimensional; incorporate financial and non-financial measures; use leading and lagging indicators; and link performance measures to the strategy of the organisation (Lord, 2007). According to Chenhall (2005), contemporary PMSs can take many forms but they share the common distinctive feature that "they are designed to present managers with financial and nonfinancial measures covering different perspectives which, in combination, provide a way of translating strategy into a coherent set of performance measures" (p. 396). Examples of contemporary PMSs include the Performance Measurement Matrix (Keegan et al., 1989), the Performance Pyramid (Lynch and Cross, 1991), the Results and Determinants Framework (Fitzgerald et al., 1991), the Balanced Scorecard (Kaplan and Norton, 1992), the Performance Prism (Neely and Adams, 2001), and the Comparative Business Scorecard (Kanji and Moura, 2002).

One of the earlier PMSs developed to reflect the need for using balanced measures was the *Performance Measurement Matrix.*[4] This framework was introduced by Keegan et al. (1989) based upon the idea that performance measures are a guide for management actions and therefore should be derived from business strategy. This framework is a response to the need of organisations to measure performance from multiple dimensions: internal, external, cost, and non-cost performance measures. In addition, the framework stresses the importance of measuring performance based on a thorough understanding of cost relationships and cost behaviour. Although this framework consists of different performance measurement dimensions and is easy to understand, it has been criticised for not including the specific organisational performance attributes required to operate in the current dynamic environment, such as the quality of services, innovation, and flexibility (Neely et al., 1995).

The *Performance Pyramid* (also known as the "Strategic Measurement Analysis and Reporting Technique" [SMART] system) presented by Wang Laboratories (Lynch and Cross, 1991) is developed from the concept of cascading measures that flow down from the organisation to the department and on to the work centre level, reflecting the corporate vision as well as internal and external business unit objectives. The four levels of the pyramid embody the corporate vision, accountability of business units, competitive dimensions for business operating systems, and specific operational criteria. Although this system considers layers between the business units and individual business activities it also combines financial, non-financial, and operational and strategic indicators. It does not, however, explicitly focus on integrating the concept of continuous improvement (Ghalayini et al., 1997).

The *Results and Determinants Framework* (Fitzgerald et al., 1991) includes lead and lag performance measures. This PMS specifically targets performance measurement in the service sector. The framework identifies six performance measures. While two of them measure the results (lagging indicators) of competitive success (competitiveness and financial performance), the other four measure the determinants (leading indicators) of competitive success (quality of service, flexibility, resource utilisation, and innovation). Fitzgerald et al. (1991) found that many service organisations have used the same criteria based on their suggested results and determinants categories. The main disadvantage of this performance framework is that it does not emphasise the causal link between the results and their determinants.

The *Balanced Scorecard (BSC)*, developed by Kaplan and Norton (1992, 1996), integrates the financial, customer, internal business process, and learning and growth perspectives. The Balanced Scorecard provides a mechanism to translate the organisation's vision and strategic goals into measurable outputs, measures, and targets. Such a process enables alignment between the business units' strategic goals and the outputs, measures, targets, and action plans. Kaplan and Norton (1992) argue that the full potential of the Balanced Scorecard will only be realised if it focuses on the functions and divisions of an organisation to position them in the context of the organisation's overall strategy. According to Kennerley and Neely (2002), the concept of the balanced scorecard is similar to Tableau de Bord, developed in the early 20th century, which establishes measures at different organisational levels.

Although the Balanced Scorecard fulfils key managerial requirements, it is criticised for not considering the interests of all stakeholders, such as suppliers, regulators, and the community (Brignall and Modell, 2000; Ghalayini and Noble, 1996; Neely et al., 1995). Norreklit (2000) states that the Balanced Scorecard is top-down driven and hence "it may be difficult to get the scorecard rooted in the employees" (p. 79). According to Meyer (2002), it does not provide guidance on how to combine dissimilar measures into an overall matrix of performance measurement within an organisation, thereby making it difficult to implement performance measures of a non-financial character.

More recently, Neely and Adams (2001) developed the *Performance Prism* to fulfil the growing importance of focusing on stakeholders' requirements when measuring performance. The Performance Prism has five perspectives: stakeholder satisfaction, strategies, processes, capabilities, and stakeholder contribution (Neely and Adams, 2001; Neely et al., 2002). In the first perspective, managers should ascertain the needs and wants of the most influential stakeholders. After determining the stakeholders, it is necessary to choose the appropriate strategies that the organisation should adopt to satisfy their needs. Performance measures are then established after identifying the strategies. The third perspective is to determine what processes need to be put in place to execute strategies. This is followed by determining the capabilities and resources required for operating these processes. The final perspective is to identify the stakeholders' contribution to maintaining and developing the capabilities. According to Neely et al. (2002), gaining an understanding of the dynamics that exist between what stakeholders want and what they contribute to the organisation can be extremely valuable for organisations.

The advantage of this framework is its ability to allow a larger group of stakeholders to be included in the performance measurement scheme (Abran and Buglione, 2003). The Performance Prism identifies the reciprocal relationship between the stakeholders and the organisation. The focus on the stakeholder contribution can be identified as a unique feature of the Performance Prism (Neely and Adams, 2001). However, Tangen (2004) argues that appropriate guidance for the selection of measures is lacking in the Performance Prism.

The most recent PMS developed is the *Comparative Business Scorecard*. This system was developed by Kanji and Moura (2002) as an improvement to the Balanced Scorecard. The authors argue that to achieve business excellence, companies need to (i) maximise stakeholders' value; (ii) achieve process excellence; (iii) improve organisational learning; and (iv) improve satisfaction of the stakeholder. Kanji and Moura (2002) suggest that, by focusing on these four elements and critical success factors, organisations can develop specific performance measures to monitor business units' performance towards excellence.

The key features of contemporary PMSs, as described in this section, are summarised in Table 2.1.

Table 2.1 Key features of contemporary performance measurement systems

Performance measurement system	*Key features*
Performance Measurement Matrix (Keegan et al., 1989)	• Integrates financial and non-financial measures • Measures aligned to business strategy • Focuses on balance in performance measurement • Measurement matrix consists of four dimensions (internal, external, cost, and non-cost performance measures) • Focus on measuring performance through cost relationships and cost behaviour
Performance Pyramid (Lynch and Cross, 1991)	• Integrates financial and non-financial measures • Measures derived from business strategy • Focuses on balance in performance measurement • Causal relationship between low-level and high level measures • Measurement matrix consists of four levels (business units, business operating units, departments, and work centres) • Integrates corporate objectives with operational measures
Results and Determinants Framework (Fitzgerald et al., 1991)	• Integrates financial and non-financial measures • Measures aligned to business strategy • Focuses on balance in performance measurement • Measurement matrix consists of two dimensions (results – competitiveness and financial performance; determinants – quality, flexibility, resource utilisation, and innovation) • Causal relationship between six category of measures • Causal relationship between professional services level, shop services level, and mass services level.

(*Continued*)

Table 2.1 (Continued)

Performance measurement system	Key features
Balanced Scorecard (Kaplan and Norton, 1992, 1996)	• Integrates financial and non-financial measures • Measures aligned to business strategy and vision • Focuses on balance in performance measurement • Measurement matrix consists of four perspectives (financial, customer, internal business process, and learning and growth) • Lead and lag measures • Internal and external measures • Causal relationship between four perspectives • Top management driven
Performance Prism (Neely and Adams, 2001)	• Integrates financial and non-financial measures, and measures of efficiency and effectiveness • Measures aligned to business strategy • Focuses on balance in performance measurement • Process oriented • Prism consists of five perspectives (stakeholder satisfaction, strategies, processes, capabilities, and stakeholder contributions)
Comparative Business Scorecard (Kanji and Moura, 2002)	• Measures derived from strategy • Link operations with strategic objectives • Process oriented • Measurement matrix consists of quality, flexibility, time, finance, and customer satisfaction

2.2.3 *The adoption of contemporary performance measurement systems*

Empirical evidence suggests that, by the end of the 1990s, most organisations had begun to move towards the use of contemporary PMSs (Neely et al., 2002; Pun and White, 2005). Fifty per cent of organisations in North America and forty per cent in Europe significantly changed their measurement practices (Frigo and Krumwiede, 1999). In Australia, McCunn (1998) found that thirty per cent of the top 1,000 organisations had adopted contemporary PMSs. Additionally, a survey conducted in the United States in 1998 showed that forty-three per cent of the 276 companies surveyed had abandoned their traditional PMSs with the majority adopting the Balanced Scorecard (Rigby, 2001). Silk (1998) found that sixty per cent of "Fortune 500" firms in the United States had experimented with new PMSs. A similar research conducted by the Gartner Group also indicates that over fifty per cent of large United States organisations had adopted a new PMS (in this case the Balanced Scorecard) by the end of 2000 (Downing, 2001). Chow et al. (1997) found that eighty per cent of large United States-based organisations were interested in changing their PMSs to meet the demands of the 2lst century. Providing evidence in the context of an emerging economy, Anand et al. (2005) found that forty-five per cent of the private and multinational companies operating in India had adopted the Balanced Scorecard by the end of 2002.

Similarly, in 2001 the Cost Management Interest Group of the Institute of Management Accountants conducted a survey of its 1,300 members on performance measurement practices and reported that eighty per cent of its respondents reported making changes to their PMS during the previous three years (Krumwiede and Charles, 2006). The changes ranged from discontinuation of an existing PMS to adding or deleting performance measures and refining the mix of measures. The survey found that thirty-three per cent of the changes were required due to organisational restructuring initiatives. The joint survey conducted by the American Institute of Certified Public Accountants and Maisel (2001), which included 1,990 respondents, found that only thirty-five per cent of respondents considered their existing PMSs (traditional PMSs in this case) to be effective, while eighty per cent of respondents indicated their intention to change their existing PMS in the near future (AICPA and Maisel, 2001).

While the above studies suggest that there is an increase in the use of contemporary PMSs, traditional PMSs are still being used (Perera et al., 2007; Chan, 2004). This may be because PMS change decisions are not made in isolation but are influenced by a variety of internal and external factors that could either facilitate or inhibit PMS change. The internal factors typically include changes in business strategy and structure, extended hierarchies and greater decentralisation, changes in budgeting and budgetary control practices, increasingly diversified product lines, and the need for more information (Chenhall, 2005; Wagner et al., 2001; Homburg et al., 1999; Chenhall and Morris, 1995; Dunk, 1992; Merchant, 1984; Miles and Snow, 1978; Khandwalla, 1972). The external factors generally include increased competition, technological innovations, environmental uncertainty and hostility, and highly challenging and continuously changing regulatory demands such as deregulation (PriceWaterhouseCoopers, 2009; Bourne et al., 2003; Hartmann, 2000; Chenhall, 2003; Anderson and Lanen, 1999; Chapman, 1997; O'Connor, 1995; Merchant, 1990; Hofstede, 1984; Khandwalla, 1977). The influence of these factors on organisations could lead to differences in the nature and the use of PMSs within organisations. It follows that organisations which experience changes in relation to their environments are likely to introduce changes in their PMSs. Damanpour and Evan (1984, p. 35) in this context suggest that:

> As the environment changes the structure or processes of the organisation undergo change to meet the new environment conditions. Innovative organisations tend to do more. They not only adapt to the environment changes, but also use their resources and skills to create new environment conditions, e.g. by introducing new products or services never offered previously. Innovations are means of providing these internal and external changes and are, therefore, a means of maintaining or improving organisational performance.

The success of an organisation depends on its ability to adapt to change (Burns and Scapens, 2000). Modell (2007) suggests that changes in the organisational environment generate pressures that influence management accounting systems. To survive, organisations must continuously change and reinvent themselves with new, improved, and relevant systems and procedures, including PMSs. As emphasised earlier, PMSs become redundant over time and lose utility if they are not able to adapt to the changes in the environment (Bourne et al., 2003; Eccles, 1998; Johnson and Kaplan, 1987). With this perspective in mind, the next section discusses how changes in the organisational environment have had implications for PMSs.

2.3 Changes in performance measurement systems

A substantial body of literature has focused on examining changes in the broader concept of management accounting systems with a number of studies referring to the PMS as a part of the management accounting system (e.g., Modell, 2007; Chan, 2004; Wickramasinghe et al., 2004; Bourne et al., 2003; Chenhall, 2005; Kasurinen, 2002; Helliar et al., 2002; Hussain and Hoque, 2002; Cobb et al., 1995; Innes and Mitchell, 1990). The literature in this area mainly relates to the manufacturing sector in developed economies and focuses on "how" change occurs (e.g., Chenhall and Euske, 2007; Soin et al., 2002; Burns and Vaivio, 2001; Soin, 1996), "who" drives or initiates change (e.g., Hussain and Hoque, 2002; Greenwood and Hinings, 1996; Cobb et al., 1995), and "what" factors influence and impede change (e.g., Kennerley and Neely, 2002; Kasurinen, 2002; Frei et al., 1998; Neely et al., 1995; Innes and Mitchell, 1990).

These studies imply that change is the product of ideas, values, and beliefs that originate in an organisational environment (Greenwood and Hinings, 1996). Accordingly, given PMSs operate within the unique situational settings of organisations, which, in turn, operate within their broader external environment, the external environment can affect the appropriateness of their performance measurement practices. Examples of these external environmental factors include uncertain and poor economic and political conditions (Baines and Langfield-Smith, 2003; Hussain and Hoque, 2002; Reid and Smith, 1999), growing competition (Hoque and James, 2000; Libby and Waterhouse, 1996; Innes and Mitchell, 1990), changes in technology (Abernethy et al., 2004; Baines and Langfield-Smith, 2003), socio-cultural conditions (Efferin and Hopper, 2007; Wickramasinghe and Hopper, 2005; Hussain and Hoque, 2002; Uddin and Hopper, 2001; Firth, 1996), and changes in government laws and regulations (Helliar et al., 2002; Cobb et al., 1995).[5] These factors and their impact on the functioning of organisations are discussed in detail in Chapter 3, while developing the analytical framework for the research.

It has been widely recognised in the management accounting literature that external environmental factors can create pressures that organisations must adapt to in order to survive and prosper (Chenhall, 2005). DiMaggio and Powell (1991) with Meyer and Rowan (1977) suggest that the pressures that emanate from the changes in the external environment stimulate changes in structures, systems, and strategies of an organisation which, in turn, lead to either the adoption of innovative PMSs, the modification of existing PMSs, or, at times, more rigorous use of existing PMSs (Kasurinen, 2002; Greenwood and Hinings, 1996; Cobb et al., 1995). This implies that the type and nature of the PMS used by an organisation varies according to the pressures generated from the environment within which it operates. For instance, banks function under the central bank's regulations and these regulations depend on a country's overall economic conditions. Under uncertain economic conditions, central banks would increase the number of regulatory controls and encourage banks to make greater use of financial measures for assessing performance (PriceWaterhouseCoopers, 2009; Hussain and Hoque, 2002).

Eccles (1991) highlighted that organisations have become increasingly keen to introduce better PMSs in order to deal with the demands of intensive global competition. The increased competition has forced organisations to devote more attention to improving customer service with many organisations improving the quality of their products and services. At the same time organisations have changed their PMSs by adopting performance measures which assist in assessing more qualitative aspects of organisational performance such as quality and customer satisfaction. To survive in a highly competitive environment, organisations are required to analyse their PMSs continuously to remove inappropriate or obsolete measures (Bourne et al., 2000) and to ensure that appropriate measures are used to strengthen the link between business processes and strategies in order to achieve organisational goals (Eccles, 1991).

Further, Eccles (1991) notes that organisations are subject to regulatory demands to achieve certain performance standards. For instance, in the banking industry, banks are expected to maintain a minimum capital adequacy and liquidity level to meet the conditions of the Basel Accords. These regulations have required banks to change their PMSs to accommodate these conditions by adding new measures to assess capital adequacy and liquidity. Eccles (1991) also notes that new technology has provided the potential to enhance the performance measurement function within organisations by capturing data which previously had been difficult to access. Similarly, Bititci et al. (2002) and Ittner and Larcker (1998) indicate that changes in technology have enabled organisations worldwide to apply performance measures such as quality, productivity, deliverability, and flexibility in order to cope with the challenges emerging from the changing business environment. In a similar vein, Hussain and Hoque (2002) suggest that changes in PMSs are mainly due to the development of new technologies, the increasing complexity of markets, and future uncertainty. They further indicate that the influence of these factors on organisations is likely to lead to differences in the nature and the use of PMSs across organisations.

It is also apparent from the literature that certain organisational factors could provide the impetus for changes in PMSs. Jones (1985), in this context, demonstrates how a change in organisational ownership following an acquisition/merger is an event with wide-ranging implications for management accounting systems, such as PMSs. For instance, a new dominant partner may import its performance measurement methods into its new entity in an attempt to enable uniformity of methods such as performance reporting in the new entity. Other forms of organisational restructuring such as those involving alterations in the level of decentralisation, hierarchical structure, downsizing, and outsourcing have also been identified as being implicated in PMS change (Shields, 1995; Burns et al., 1999). Recent corporate failures, such as Northern Rock, Bear Stearns, Lehman Brothers, and Merrill Lynch, have sparked considerable organisational level changes to enhance corporate governance. One implication of this has been the impact on the information demands by the Board of Directors in respect to the performance of management. As a result, a PMS may have to be modified to supply, in terms of content and frequency of performance, related information which will allow the Board of Directors to discharge its duties.

The existing literature also argues that the factors that influence changes in PMSs are not always independent and that the influence of each environmental factor on a PMS may not be direct, but rather by way of another environmental factor. For example, while organisational structure and regulatory change have been presented in the literature as factors that could influence change independently, a change in organisational structure, which influences changes in PMSs, could itself have been driven by the regulatory changes experienced by the organisation (De Waal, 2007; Kasurinen, 2002; Brignall and Modell, 2000). It means that the changes in the organisational environment in which the organisation operates could influence changes in PMSs, directly as well as indirectly.

The nature and degree of changes in a PMS may take various forms such as the introduction of new performance measures, deleting or discarding existing performance measures, or increased usage of existing PMSs (Bititci et al., 2000; Banker et al., 1993). Irrespective of the nature and the degree of change in organisational environment, the intensity of change in the PMS often depends on the reaction of organisational members to the pressures for change generated by the organisational environment (Ang and Cummings, 1997). The relative inflexibility and rigidity of organisational members with respect to change makes it both difficult and problematic (Brignall and Modell, 2000). Further, due to the complexity of existing allied systems and procedures, the change process may not proceed as intended (Bourne et al., 2003; Kaplan and Norton, 1996; Neely et al., 1995). To make a successful PMS change, it is therefore important for organisations to examine the context of change carefully, particularly its impact on other allied systems and procedures, and to manage the reaction of the organisational members so that changes in the PMS are implemented within the organisation's norms and values (Soin et al., 2002). The next subsection discusses the literature concerning the potential reactions to PMS change.

2.3.1 *Potential reactions to changes in performance measurement systems*

A review of the management accounting literature suggests that changes in management accounting systems, such as PMSs, have the potential to trigger positive as well as negative reactions from employees (Kasurinen, 2002; Burns and Scapens, 2000; Scapens and Roberts, 1993). According to Dent and Goldberg (1999), organisational members' positive reactions toward change immensely facilitate the achievement of intended outcomes of the change process. On the other hand, negative reactions to change may cause frustration and confusion which could impede the process of change (Vaivio, 1999; Scapens and Roberts, 1993).

Burns and Scapens (2000) define resistance as "reluctance to conform to new modes of thinking and behaviour, either by choice or through difficulty in adapting" (p. 16). Kasurinen (2002) maintains that existing institutions, such as structure, cultural values, and norms, can act as barriers to change.[6] Since institutions exist outside the awareness of organisational members, they become filters of what is perceived and thought about by organisational members (Burns and Scapens, 2000). For instance, a change in the PMS can be interpreted by the organisational members as disrupting and affecting their work routines. Hence, changes that are not congruent with existing institutions are likely to be resisted, formally or informally (Dent and Goldberg, 1999).

Burns and Scapens (2000) indicate that resistance to changes in PMSs could be formal and overt. It could be due to the organisational members not having the capacity or knowledge to implement change, and/or could arise from mental allergies to specific ways of thinking and doing things within the organisation. Modell (2007) suggests that whatever is the nature of the resistance an organisation faces, it could lead to considerable anxiety and confusion for organisational members. Scapens and Roberts (1993) maintain that an organisational member's inability or unwillingness to understand consequences of change or a lack of understanding the reasons for change may lead to resistance to changes in management accounting systems, such as PMSs. They note that such reactions should not be ignored because resistance could not only cause delays in changes in management accounting systems, but could also bring unintended outcomes including the decision to abandon the change altogether.

When there is a possibility of resistance to change, the initiators of changes to the PMS may have to force through their implementation (Kasurinen, 2002). This might be through the use of hierarchical power or by obtaining the backing of those with sufficient power to force the change. Those introducing changes in the PMS also have the power because they control the detail of the PMS change process (Kasurinen, 2002). Burns and Scapens (2000) maintain that the use of hierarchical power alone cannot ensure a successful change in the PMS. If there is no adequate review system during the change process, or the change in the PMS depends on the support and resources of those who resist the change, then organisational members may be able to modify the PMS in accordance with their existing institutions (Modell, 2007). In such circumstances, power lies not only with senior management, but also junior management who can actively react to the change (Cobb et al., 1995). They might be able to subvert the changes in the PMS, for instance, through modifying the PMS in ways which are compatible with their existing ways of measuring performance.

Additionally, when organisations introduce changes in PMSs, in an attempt to reduce resistance, change facilitating factors are embedded in change endeavours

(Tsamenyi et al., 2006). These facilitating factors generally include hiring external consultants, providing training to employees, imparting the rationale behind a change, and engaging employees in the change process. While describing factors that facilitate PMS change, Bourne et al. (2002) pointed out that the expression of the purpose of PMS change and having higher level or top management commitment are important factors for a successful change. In a similar context, McAdam et al. (2005), in their research of the development of a PMS in a large UK public sector department, showed that despite the broad acceptance among organisational members at all levels, the PMS change failed due to the lack of training. They suggested building continuous training and improvement processes into the PMS in order to succeed with change.

Radnor and Lovell (2003) emphasise the importance of creating a culture for performance measurement before the change is initiated. They also claim that the organisation's history in terms of performance measurement and resources designated for the PMS change efforts may also influence the outcome of the change. Implementing such facilitating measures seems to be crucial because the effectiveness of changes and the consequential response to change pressures depends on those who are directly affected by the change (Siti-Nabiha and Scapens, 2005; Shields and Young, 1989).

2.4 Performance measurement practices in banks

The banking sector is the most dominant economic sector in modern societies (Frei et al., 1998). In the most advanced countries, like Australia, its contribution accounts for almost five per cent of the Gross Domestic Product (Reserve Bank of Australia, 2010). In emerging economies, particularly those economies that are aspiring to make their presence in international financial markets, the contribution of the banking sector is even more significant. For instance, the banking sector in countries like India, Pakistan, and Bangladesh accounts for over seven per cent of the country's Gross Domestic Product (World Bank, 2009, 2010). These statistics suggest that banks play an important role in an economy as intermediaries between depositors/investors and borrowers of capital. Banks' core business activities generate two sources of income, i.e., interest/mark-up earnings and incomes from fees/commissions. Their operations are usually distinguished in terms of the different natures of banking activities, such as commercial banking, corporate banking, investment banking, private banking, electronic banking, and domestic and international trade finance. While some banks specialise in one or more of these areas, universal banks usually cover all of the outlined activities.[7]

Until the 1970s, banks worldwide operated in a highly stable environment with low interest rates, regulated rates for deposits, and relatively predictable yield curves (Harker and Zenios, 1998). Their income was guaranteed with substantial interest spreads (Fries and Taci, 2005).[8] The need to monitor performance in relation to costs and the profitability of banks' business activities was not that important, and as a consequence the internal control and performance measurement practices of banks were loosely developed (Bonin et al., 2004; Fries et al., 2002). External financial reports, such as reports submitted to the regulators, were considered sufficient for banks to measure the performance of their business activities (Jeucken and Bouma, 1999).

Progressive deregulation in the 1980s coupled with the stringent capital requirements of the Basel Accords has changed the risk profile of banks (Lapavitsas and Santos, 2008). In recent years, the structure of banks has evolved into focused and semi-autonomous lines of business, each with a different product, customer, distribution, or geographic mandate (Helliar et al., 2002; Karr, 1997; Kimball, 1997). This decentralised organisational structure has raised issues concerning performance measurement within banks (Karr, 1997). For example, the increasing operational responsibilities of managers in bank branches, the diversification in product lines, and the increased role of e-banking products and services have forced banks to strengthen their internal controls, including PMSs (Bank for International Settlements, 2006).

Moreover, PriceWaterhouseCoopers (2009) and the Bank for International Settlements (2006) highlight that, following the rapid change in the banking environment over the last two decades, banks worldwide have realised that they lack the information that enables them to measure performance accurately, mitigate risk, and inculcate internal controls across different business areas. For instance, anecdotal evidence shows that a number of banks in the US and Europe suffered financial losses primarily because of breakdowns in internal controls and the lack of information available due to inadequate and ineffective performance measurement and risk management systems (Helliar et al., 2002). In response to these changes, banks have developed and adopted a number of innovative and robust solutions to improve controls and their PMSs, including new databases and new analytical ways to prudently assess costs, benefits, and risks (Fries and Taci, 2005; Karr, 1997).

The review of the banking literature also demonstrates that banks have been under immense pressure from regulatory bodies since the implementations of the Basel Accords of the Bank for International Settlements in 1988 (Bank for International Settlements, 2001). These Accords explicitly assert that banks must develop adequate systems for measuring and controlling their business activities. These Accords also assert that top management and the Board of Directors should receive performance-related information on a regular basis to mitigate potential risks and losses that could affect the operations of the bank. In compliance with the Basel Accords requirements, according to the Bank for International Settlements (2001), a number of banks are measuring the performance of their business activities across multiple dimensions. In particular, besides using financial measures such as the quality of assets, the quality of management, liquidity and capital adequacy, earning performance, and monitoring risks, banks also focus on using non-financial measures (Bank for International Settlements, 2001, p. 7).

The review of the performance measurement literature suggests that the focus of the existing literature examining changes in PMSs has largely been on manufacturing organisations, with little attention paid to banking institutions. Banks differ from manufacturing organisations (Cobb et al., 1995; Drury and Tyles,

1995) with Fitzgerald et al. (1991) suggesting that most products and services of banking institutions, unlike manufacturing, are *intangible* and *perishable* as they cannot be stored. Further, the production and consumption of banking products and services are *simultaneous* and *heterogeneous*. These distinctions, as suggested by Fitzgerald et al. (1991), could lead to differences in the nature of control systems and performance measurement practices between banks and manufacturing organisations.

A review of the banking literature also suggests that control systems and performance measurement practices in banks vary significantly from manufacturing organisations because in banks these systems are strongly influenced by regulatory systems. For instance, banks operate under their national regulatory bodies, such as the central bank, and these regulatory bodies are expected to implement control systems and procedures framed by international financial institutions, in particular, the Bank for International Settlements. The Bank for International Settlements issues guidelines for effective internal controls and measurement practices to encourage safe and sound operations in banks. The Bank for International Settlements also ensures that banks maintain reliable financial and managerial reporting. Further, banks are expected to maintain minimum financial standards to maintain capital adequacy and liquidity in accordance with international regulatory standards (Frei et al., 1998).[9]

Furthermore, it is critical that banks meet very high standards of confidentiality and security. Frei et al. (1998) further suggest that in sharp contrast to manufacturing organisations, banks invest heavily in new technologies to meet the demands of customers for high quality services due to the unique nature of their operational activities. Banks often do not just want information about product and service costs; they also want to know which customers are profitable and which customers are not. Such information enables banks to quantify the value of each customer and focus on capturing, retaining, and developing relationships with their most valuable customers. Further, as banks maintain close contact and relationships with their customers, the efficiency and effectiveness of their systems and procedures are of paramount importance (Helliar et al., 2002). This has a direct impact on the information flow and the scope of information systems used to support a PMS.

Considering the differences between banks and manufacturing organisations in terms of the nature of their business operations, the technology they use, and regulatory requirements, it is inferred that the factors that influence changes in PMSs within banks could also be different. Further, their responses to the pressures they face could also be different when compared with manufacturing organisations because of the different nature of their institutional environment. This research contends that banks may not simply acquiesce to the influence of environmental factors. Rather, their response could vary from a simple conformance to active resistance. However, their response to the pressure to change depends on the nature as well as the degree and intensity of the pressures generated in their environment. Researching such a notion of change in the PMS within banks has largely been ignored in the management accounting literature (Greenwood and Hinings, 1996). Hence, the foregoing discussions and literature support the current research's focus on examining the potential influence of the factors that influence changes in PMSs within banks, and investigating the responses to the change pressures that emanate from their environment. Further, an understanding of the way in which banks respond to pressures could help in implementing more effective changes in PMSs.

In addition, the review of the management accounting literature suggests that studies that have examined the phenomena of PMS change have examined organisations operating in developed countries with limited empirical evidence on such changes within emerging economies (Waweru et al., 2004; O'Connor et al., 2004; Firth, 1996; Hoque and Hopper, 1994, 1997). Waweru et al. (2004) suggest that emerging economies face unique political, social, economic, and regulatory conditions that play a vital role in causing change within organisations. Hoque and Hopper (1997), for example, found that macro-level factors such as political climate, government legislation, industrial relations, and aid agencies influenced systems related to budgetary procedures (e.g., budget evaluation, participation, flexibility) in a Bangladesh company. While research on emerging markets has increased over the past couple of years, this research does not explicitly offer solid grounds to conclude why and how management accounting systems such as PMSs change in emerging economies (Uddin and Hopper, 2001). Consequently, calls have been made to understand better the change phenomena in management accounting systems (such as PMSs) in the context of emerging economies (Waweru et al., 2004; Uddin and Hopper, 2001; Firth, 1996).

The above review of the literature demonstrates that the studies that have examined the influence of organisational environment on management accounting systems such as PMSs have largely referred to the performance measurement practices in manufacturing organisations with few studies on banking institutions (e.g., Guerreiro et al., 2006; Soin et al., 2002; Hussain and Hoque, 2002; Cobb et al., 1995). The literature review also reveals that these studies are largely limited to developed countries (e.g., Helliar et al., 2002; Hussain and Hoque, 2002; Soin, 1996; Frei et al., 1998; Cobb et al., 1995).

The above discussion asserts the need and importance of developing an analytical framework that can facilitate a comprehensive analysis of PMS change. Accordingly, the next chapter (Chapter 3) will develop an analytical framework for this research to provide a better explanation of the underlying phenomenon of this research. The framework will focus on the factors that influence change in PMSs and the responses to change efforts within the context of the banking institutions in emerging economies.

2.5 Summary

This chapter presented a review of the literature concerning PMSs, including a discussion of the nature, purposes, and uses of PMSs. The chapter also reviewed the literature concerning changes in PMSs in general and the banking sector in particular. The literature review suggests that there is a general agreement about the inadequacy of traditional financial-based PMSs and the need to change PMSs to cope with changes in the organisational environment including increased competition, new management practices, regulatory changes, and continuous improvement in technologies. Consequently, over the last couple of decades there have been numerous attempts to develop new measurement systems that overcome the limitations of traditional PMSs and also a tendency for organisations to change their existing financially based PMSs and adopt those measurement systems (e.g., Krumwiede and Charles, 2006; Bourne et al., 2003; AICPA and Maisel, 2001; Frigo and Krumwiede, 1999; Drury et al., 1993).

Most of the studies conducted to understand why and how PMSs change focus on manufacturing organisations and their findings are not applicable to banking institutions due to the significant differences in these two sectors. The few studies (e.g., Soin et al., 2002; Hussain and Hoque, 2002; Helliar et al., 2002; Cobb et al., 1995) which do investigate issues concerning PMSs were undertaken in banks operating in developed countries. Furthermore, these studies have failed to examine factors that influence PMS change and the responses to the pressures that force such change.

Notes

1 'Performance' can be measured in terms of inputs (efficiency and effectiveness of resources used), outputs (products and services produced), and outcomes (Neely et al., 1995).
2 Melnyk et al. (2004) define a metric as a measure that consists of three elements: (i) the specific measure (what is being measured); (ii) the standard (the numerical value that identifies the minimum threshold of performance, as captured by the measure, considered acceptable to management); and (iii) the environment or context within which the activity is measured.
3 Since financial performance measures have been used for performance measurement purposes for decades prior to the development of multidimensional PMSs (such as the Balanced Scorecard) they are referred to as traditional PMSs (or conventional PMSs) in the management accounting literature.
4 The term balanced measures is used in the management accounting literature to refer to a combination of financial and non-financial performance measures.
5 The categorisation of technology as an external environmental factor, as opposed to an internal organisational factor, is subject to debate. While existing technology within organisations constitutes an internal organisational factor, using Waterhouse and Tiessen's (1978) explanation, change or innovation in technology normally initiates outside organisations. Therefore, for the purposes of this research, technology is considered as an external environmental factor.
6 The terms barrier, reaction, and resistance are used interchangeably at many places in this research, and refer to the same meaning.
7 Universal banks provide investment banking services in addition to services related to savings, loans (both retail and corporate loans), project finance, and fund management (Edwards and Ogilvie, 1996).
8 Interest spread is the difference between the average lending rate and the average borrowing rate for a bank (Gormley, 2007).
9 For instance, under Basel Accord II banks are required to maintain a minimum capital at eight per cent of risk-weighted assets.

3   Analytical framework

3.1 Introduction

The purpose of this chapter is to develop an analytical framework to examine changes in the performance measurement system (PMS) of the bank investigated in this book. The analytical framework presented in this chapter draws insights to understanding PMS change from an institutional theory perspective in general and, more specifically, the theoretical constructs of institutional isomorphism (DiMaggio and Powell, 1983) and Oliver's (1991) continuum of strategic responses to institutional pressures.

The chapter is divided into eight sections. Section 3.2 describes the theoretical underpinning and reasons for choosing institutional theory. Section 3.3 then explains the New Institutional Sociology strand of institutional theory and how New Institutional Sociology can be used to inform studies of PMS change. Section 3.4 provides a detailed overview of the environmental factors that could affect the functioning of banks. Section 3.5 then outlines the institutional pressures for change followed by a discussion on the strategic responses to these institutional pressures in Section 3.6. Section 3.7 presents the analytical framework that will be used to examine changes in the PMSs in the case organisation. Finally, Section 3.8 provides a summary of the chapter.

3.2 Theoretical underpinning

Institutional theory has been widely used in the fields of economics, sociology, political science, and accounting (Scott, 1995). The theory is built on the notion that organisations are influenced by forces which lie beyond their control (DiMaggio and Powell, 1983; Hoffman, 1999). Scott (1998, p. 12) comments that:

> Every organisation exists in a specific physical, technological, cultural and social environment to which it must adapt. No organisation is self-sufficient, all depend for survival on types of relations they establish with larger systems of which they are a part.

Institutional theory argues that an organisation is an open system (Scott, 1998), and its participants play a critical role in shaping organisational systems and procedures. Farrell (1996, p. 124) notes that "organisations are portrayed as being deeply embedded in, and constituted by, the environment in which they operate". The theory further asserts that organisations must adapt to environmental changes if they are to receive legitimacy and continued societal support.[1] It implies that the changes in the organisational environment are viewed as defining not only the appropriate systems and procedures that the organisation must adopt but also the manner in which it conforms to society's institutionalised beliefs.

Institutional theory has largely been based on the theoretical perspective that broadly describes management accounting systems as social institutions that are embedded in an institutional environment (Covaleski and Dirsmith, 1988; Carruthers, 1995).[2] The institutional environment is defined as regulatory structures, government agencies, laws, professions, and public opinions (Oliver, 1991, p. 147) that have the ability to exert pressures on organisations and their members (Scott, 1987). Institutional pressures compel organisations to adopt certain systems and procedures if they are to be seen as a good member of a particular industry (Barley and Tolbert, 1997). Hence, if an organisation is willing to be a legitimate member of a particular group of organisations in the same industry, it has to inculcate or conform to industry norms and values, and the expectations of society at large (Meyer and Rowan, 1977; DiMaggio and Powell, 1983; Oliver, 1991).[3] DiMaggio and Powell (1983) emphasised that the impact of institutional pressure is dependent on the position of a particular organisation within an organisational field. Over time, organisational fields are subject to change (Greenwood and Hinings, 1996).

Several studies have adopted institutional theory to examine management accounting change. While some of them have examined the influence of the institutional environment in shaping management accounting systems (e.g., Tsamenyi et al., 2006; Abernethy and Chua, 1996; Covaleski et al., 1993), others have viewed management accounting systems as internally created institutions and have investigated changes in management accounting systems as an institution in its own right (e.g., Burns and Scapens, 2000). For example, Covaleski and Dirsmith (1988) examined how budgeting systems were changed and identified those participants involved in influencing the change process. Specifically, the research focused on how institutional actors (e.g., State Department of Administration, Legislative Fiscal Bureau, the governor, campus chancellors, and deans) were able to create and enforce institutional pressures on the organisation. Hoque and Alam (1999) drew on institutional theory to account for the market pressures that influenced the adoption of total quality management and changes in the management accounting systems of a New Zealand construction company. Hussain and Hoque (2002) used an institutional theory perspective to inform a field research of non-financial performance measurement practices in four Japanese banks while Tsamenyi et al. (2006) used institutional theory to investigate changes in the accounting and financial information system of a large Spanish electricity company.

Different strands of institutional theory have been used to gain insights into management accounting change (Scapens, 2006). These include: old institutional economics, which is concerned with the institutions that shape the actions and thoughts of individual human agents; new institutional economics, which refers to the structures used to govern economic transactions; and New Institutional Sociology (NIS), which is concerned with the institutions in the organisational environment that shape organisational systems, structures, and strategies. Scapens (1994) argues that the NIS perspective of institutional theory can be used to gain an understanding of management accounting change because it offers researchers richer insights into the relationships that exist between management accounting systems and other external institutions. The NIS strand of institutional theory is considered appropriate for this research because it provides suitable analytical explanations to address the issues underpinning the current research including how and why the PMS was changed in the bank investigated. Further, NIS is considered appropriate for the current research as it seeks to take into account the wider institutional environment in order to offer a richer understanding of the PMS change phenomenon.

3.3 The New Institutional Sociology strand of institutional theory

New Institutional Sociology (NIS) maintains that the behaviour of organisations is motivated by the forces within wider society. Similarly to legitimacy theory, NIS argues that organisations seek legitimacy by adhering to rules and norms that are valued by society provided that their behaviour is directed more towards environmental acceptance than technical efficiency.[4] Organisations with reduced legitimacy are forced to consider better systems and procedures (Scott, 2001; Carpenter and Feroz, 1992). The mechanism through which organisations adopt systems and procedures is termed institutional isomorphism. According to DiMaggio and Powell (1983, p. 149) isomorphism is "a constraining process that forces one unit in a population to resemble other units that face the same set of environmental conditions". DiMaggio and Powell (1983) identify three mechanisms through which institutional isomorphism occurs, each with its own antecedents – coercive, mimetic, and normative.

Coercive isomorphism is the response to "both formal and informal pressures exerted on organisations by other organisations upon which they are dependent and by cultural expectations in the society within which the organisation functions" (DiMaggio and Powell, 1983, p. 150). Organisations are forced to change their systems and procedures directly as a consequence of changing legislation. This acquiescence to pressure helps the organisation to secure economic resources and legitimacy (Meyer and Rowan, 1991). Mimetic isomorphism is the act of copying other organisations when organisations face uncertainty and "model themselves on other organisations" in order to overcome it (DiMaggio and Powell, 1983, p. 151). In particular, ambiguous organisational goals and strategies or poorly understood technologies may cause organisations to model themselves on other organisations. Scapens (1994) argues that mimetic behaviour has a conformity element, wherein organisations adopt contemporary practices to legitimise their systems and procedures by appearing to be in control. Normative isomorphism is associated with professionalisation (DiMaggio and Powell, 1983, p. 152), and arises when professionals operating in organisations are subject to pressures to conform to a set of norms, values, and rules developed by occupational and professional bodies (Abernethy and Chua, 1996). In this form of isomorphism, organisations feel obliged to adopt structures, systems, and processes that have been advocated by dominant occupational and professional groups (Burns, 2000).

Informed by DiMaggio and Powell's (1983) notion of institutional isomorphism, this research argues that banks would introduce changes to their PMSs as a result of these three forms of pressure. However, DiMaggio and Powell's (1983) notion of institutional isomorphism does not address the possible organisational responses to efforts at making changes (Oliver, 1991) and the strategic behaviours associated with the consequential change (Covaleski and Dirsmith, 1988). Consequently, there have been calls from management accounting researchers advocating the extension of DiMaggio and Powell's (1983) notion of institutional isomorphism to include responses to the institutional pressures to change (e.g., Greenwood and Hinings, 1996).

Oliver (1991) discusses the various strategies that organisations adopt in response to institutional pressures to change. While questioning the notion of institutional determinism, she argues that organisations respond to their environment by attempting to drive it in differing directions due to diverse norms and expectations. Accordingly, conforming to institutional pressures is not an exclusive option, even if it might be tempting in order to gain legitimacy. The possibility of achieving gains through resistance is also put forward (Oliver, 1991). Thus, it is argued that an organisation makes an active response to institutional pressures with the extreme option being to either conform or resist. Oliver (1991) presented a continuum of strategic responses with five types of responses, namely, acquiescence, compromise, avoidance, defiance, and manipulation.[5]

Using the theoretical notions in both DiMaggio and Powell (1983) and Oliver (1991), this chapter develops an analytical framework to facilitate an analysis of the factors that influence changes in PMSs and the responses to change efforts. The framework identifies a number of macro-level factors that affect the functioning of banks and the resulting institutional pressures which could lead to changes in their PMSs. The framework also recognises the influence of strategic responses when introducing change with the direction, nature, and outcome of change efforts likely to be determined by the responses of the key organisational actors. The external environmental factors that could have an impact on PMSs, and the institutional pressures that could lead to changes in PMS, are discussed in Sections 3.4 and 3.5 respectively, with the strategic responses of organisations to such changes discussed in Section 3.6.

3.4 External environment factors that affect the functioning of banks

The literature suggests that changes in PMSs are influenced mainly by the macro-level environment in which banks operate (Hussain and Hoque, 2002), with the resulting changes often improving not only the quality of information, thereby leading to increased productivity and accountability (Perera, 2004), but also the ability of the organisation to survive in a highly competitive environment (Helliar et al., 2002; Cobb et al., 1995). The macro-level environment is an outer realm of banks which is outside their control. Innovations in management philosophies, trade liberalisation, new technologies, increased competition, changes in regulatory frameworks, and economic and political conditions have often been cited in the literature as major macro-level environmental factors that influence the functioning of banks (Helliar et al., 2002). This research combines these macro-level factors into three categories, namely, economic conditions, technological innovations, and the socio-cultural and political environment.

3.4.1 *Economic conditions*

In recent years, banks have faced an uncertain economic climate due to macro-economic factors such as globalisation, liberalised deregulation, privatisation, and highly fluctuating and, at times, unpredictable inflation and interest rates (Helliar et al., 2002; Harker and Zenios, 1998). Such economic conditions place pressure on banks to improve performance (Williams and Seaman, 2002; Burney, 1999), and one of the responses to such pressures appears to be to focus on the efficient and effective use of control systems, such as PMSs. For instance, the recent global financial crisis has forced banks to strengthen their PMS and internal controls by adopting risk measurement and mitigation frameworks, and strategic planning and performance reporting systems which enable each business area to monitor its contribution, and deliver clearer, relevant, and more consistent performance information (Bank of England, 2008).

Anecdotal evidence suggests that volatile market conditions (e.g., fluctuations in interest rates, foreign exchange rates, and equity prices) generate high risk for banks and threaten their earnings, capital, liquidity, and solvency. Effective risk management within banks demands accurate and timely risk quantification which can be assisted by an efficient PMS[6] (Bank of England, 2008). Therefore, banks need more formal, detailed PMSs, that not only establish stringent internal controls, but also facilitate prudent analysis which captures activities that expose banks to risk, and also measures the specific risks presented.

A review of the literature also suggests that progressive liberalisation, both within countries and across national boundaries, has led to cut-throat competition between banks and other financial institutions (Hawkins and Mihaljek, 2001). For example, GE Capital, the financial services subsidiary of General Electric and Tesco, now offers financial services including credit cards, loans, and insurance. Hence, the traditional financial intermediation role of banks to provide loans and mobilise deposits has become a relatively less important part of the overall business as banks are attempting to redefine their businesses and diversifying into a wider range of services (Lapavitsas and Santos, 2008).

Further, following the removal of ceilings on deposit rates coupled with the lifting of restrictions on domestic and foreign entry in many countries worldwide, banks have been facing increased competition (Claessens and Laeven, 2003; Hawkins and Mihaljek, 2001). Such deregulation has reduced sources of cheap funds for banks and put pressure on their profits, thereby forcing them to price their services more realistically, and charge explicitly for services previously provided free of charge (Berger, 2003; Hawkins and Mihaljek, 2001). The increased competition in the banking sector has not only enabled the access of organisations and individuals to financial services and financing, but also eroded the market share of many banks. Consequently, a substantial number of banks are entering into high-risk business ventures and off-balance sheet activities. Such activities create a need to apply appropriate internal controls and to integrate them with performance measurement practices, thereby enabling banks to tightly control and monitor their business processes (Bank for International Settlements, 2009).

The easing of restrictions on the entry of foreign banks and the search for global markets for profit opportunities has also led to the growing presence of foreign-owned banks in many countries (Gormley, 2007; World Bank, 2005, 2006). Foreign banks have introduced a range of contemporary banking technologies that focus on credit, automated credit scoring, mass distribution channels and electronic lending platforms, such as credit card networks (World Bank, 2006). They have been able to compete successfully against domestic banks, partly due to their superior usage of technology and better customer service (Lapavitsas and Santos, 2008; Hitt and Frei, 2002). Notable examples of such banks include Citibank, Hong Kong and Shanghai Banking Corporation (HSBC), and Standard Chartered Bank.

The need for more comprehensive PMSs to assist organisations to operate effectively in today's competitive environment has often been emphasised by management accounting researchers (e.g., Ferreira and Otley, 2009; Chenhall and Euske, 2007; Sulaiman and Mitchell, 2005) and practitioners (Bank of England, 2006; Bank for International Settlements, 2005). A number of recent studies have also concluded that traditional PMSs are inadequate given today's complex economic conditions (e.g., Langfield-Smith et al., 2009; Ittner and Larcker, 1998; Eccles, 1991). Such economic conditions are considered to be an influential factor in regard to the changes in the PMSs of banks.

3.4.2 *Technological innovations*

The impact of technology on management accounting practices, including performance measurement practices, has been well recognised in the management accounting literature (e.g., Garengo et al., 2007; Bititci et al., 2004; Otley, 1994; Johnson and Kaplan, 1987) with Kaplan and Norton (1996) arguing that the impact of information technology is even more revolutionary for service organisations. Technology provides an opportunity for banks to improve service performance in addition to providing a broader range of financial products and services. For instance, in order to stay competitive over the last two decades, there has been a phenomenal increase in the offer of e-banking or e-finance products and services by banks, such as internet banking, debit cards, e-bill payments, smart cards, and stored-value cards (Allen et al., 2002). These advancements have allowed banks to innovate customer service and delivery channels, not only to fulfil the needs of customers, but also to achieve economies of scale and to increase competitiveness (Hitt and Frei, 2002). Banks are also increasingly focusing on customer and product profitability analysis as key performance measures. Specifically, banks create existing and potential customers' profiles which they use in decisions to lend, mobilise deposits, and track movement of customers' accounts (PriceWaterhouseCoopers, 2009; Helliar et al., 2002).

Additionally, the banking literature suggests that the automation of transactions and associated developments have radically changed the operational structure of banks. For example, transactions between banks and their depositors have mostly become automated, the techniques of funds transmission have been altered, and new ways of managing accounts and making payments have emerged. These changes have contributed to a steadily rising number of Automated Teller Machines (ATMs) and online transactions, and increased pressure on banks to expand investments in complex information technology infrastructures (Berger, 2003). While these changes have created new business opportunities for banks, the changes have also significantly enhanced the risk for banks due to the enhanced volume of business activities and the increased flow of information (Bank for International Settlements, 2006). Such changes require banks to use stringent management accounting and information systems (Bititci et al., 2004). Against these trends, anecdotal evidence suggests that banks have been forced to adopt new types of control mechanisms and management procedures, including introducing performance measures, such as the number of customers per ATM, the number of transactions per ATM, the number of faulty transactions, and the number of ATM breakdowns, in order to foster control over business activities.

3.4.3 Socio-cultural and political environment

The socio-cultural and political environment is generally characterised by the rules and requirements which individual organisations must conform to if they are to gain support and legitimacy (DiMaggio and Powell, 1983). Scott (2001) suggests that political pressures generally result from changes in the interests of individuals or groups and the underlying power distributions that support the existing institutional environment. Socio-cultural pressure is associated with the differentiation of groups and the existence of heterogeneous or divergent beliefs and practices (Frank and Fahrbach, 1999). The presence of these pressures, over time, could undermine the stability of organisations, thereby contributing to the gradual abandonment of certain management practices within an organisation (Stark, 1996). For example, in many Islamic countries, banks have been forced to introduce "profit and loss based or interest free" banking products, abandoning the "interest based" products to satisfy the fundamental belief (faith) of Islamic societies which prohibits charging interest (Ahmad, 1993). Consequently, central banks in many Islamic countries have issued a separate set of prudential regulations for Islamic banking activities (Errico and Farahbaksh, 1998).

Within the banking literature it is argued that banks voluntarily, or sometimes obligatorily, follow international organisational standards/quality measurement stipulations determined by institutions, such as the Bank for International Settlements, the International Standards Organisation (ISO), and the United Nations Organization (UNO), and consequently adapt their management controls, including performance measures, to conform to the recommendation of such bodies (Holland et al., 1997; Alam, 1997; Hoque and Hopper, 1994; Hussain and Gunasekaran, 2002). For instance, the Bank for International Settlements has made it obligatory for banks operating in developing countries to adopt performance measures and internal control standards set under Basel Accords if they intend to operate in international markets. Banks in these countries have also been encouraged by the Bank for International Settlements to extensively use their PMS in order to restrain the negative impact of political and social instability. Similarly, transnational institutions like the World Trade Organization (WTO), World Health Organization (WHO), and regional blocs also encourage banks to adopt practices that are consistent with international standards and practices.

The three macro-level factors discussed in this section, namely, economic conditions, technological innovations, and the socio-cultural and political environment, seem to have a significant influence on the functioning of banks. As a result, banks generally become more competitive, resilient to technological innovations and associated service capabilities, and responsive to socio-cultural and political needs in order to secure their survival and legitimacy. Such requirements have significant implications for systems and procedures within banks, including PMSs. Nevertheless, organisational responses to macro-level influences are often not spontaneous. The nature of responses as well as the direction of responses to the influence of the macro-level factors could result from the three types of pressures (coercive, mimetic, and normative) which are discussed in the following section.

3.5 Institutional pressures to change

Institutional theory suggests that institutional pressures make organisations adapt in order to gain legitimacy (Covaleski and Dirsmith, 1988). Effective change to existing practices depends on the intensity of the institutional pressures for change and the degree of institutionalisation of existing practice (DiMaggio and Powell, 1983; Jepperson, 1991). According to Jepperson (1991), pressure to change could arise due to incongruity between existing practices and the institutional environment. For instance, if the PMS used by a bank conflicts with the expectations of the regulators, these expectations will pressure the bank to change its system in accordance with the regulatory requirements. Consistent with this view, this research argues that the pressures on banks to change their PMSs could occur in three forms, namely, coercive, mimetic, and normative. This section discusses the way in which these pressures cause banks to respond to the macro-level factors discussed in the previous section.

3.5.1 Coercive pressures

Institutional theory suggests that some institutional fields contain powerful environmental agents which impose structural forms or practices on subordinate organisational units (DiMaggio and Powell, 1983, 1991). Coercive pressures to change performance measurement practices could eventuate from other organisations upon which a particular organisation is dependent (DiMaggio and Powell, 1983). For instance, in relation to the banking sector, prior research highlights the coercive influence exerted through the central bank's regulatory control and financial legislations (Hussain, 2003; Hoque and Hopper, 1994).

Central Bank's regulatory control

Banks are required to comply with the regulations and guidelines of central banks, including the prudential regulations and the Basel Agreements. Basel Accord II describes comprehensive measures and a minimum standard for capital adequacy that supervisory authorities are required to implement through rule-making and adoption procedures. It seeks to improve the existing rules by aligning regulatory capital requirements more closely to the underlying risks that banks face. In addition, Basel Accord II was intended to promote a more forward-looking approach to capital supervision, one that encourages banks to identify the risks they may face today and in the future, and to develop or improve their ability to manage those risks.

In order to comply with Basel Accord II, central banks in a number of countries have introduced the CAMELS and CAELS frameworks[7] to evaluate banks' performance (Asian Development Bank, 2002; Hilbers et al., 2000). The failure to comply with the central bank's regulations and guidelines attracts financial penalties or cancellation of banking licences. Banks are, therefore, required to improve their performance measurement as well as internal control and risk measurement practices to be in accordance with central bank and Basel standards. The pressure to improve performance measurement will be far greater in the next few years after the implementation of Basel Accord III at the end of 2012. This Accord will require banks to: maintain higher tier-1 and tier-2 risk-weighted capital ratio; use a leverage ratio as a safety net; maintain higher liquidity; use higher risk-weightings for trading assets of the banks; and exclude most of their off-balance sheet exposures from capital (Wignall and Atkinson, 2010; Lall, 2009). Such changes in the regulatory frameworks and legislations are likely to be an influential factor in regard to the changes in management controls, including the PMSs in banks.

Financial legislation

Accounting bodies such as the Financial Accounting Standard Board (FASB) in the US and the International Accounting Standard Board (IASB) in the UK prescribe accounting standards, which in turn impact on the accounting systems which PMSs rely upon. Central banks require banks to follow the accounting standards and International Statements of Auditing (ISAs) and Audit Codes issued by the International Federation of Accountants (IFAC). Basel Accord II requires that banks implement a progressive adaptation of risk evaluation techniques. This has forced banks to transform their existing systems and procedures to accommodate the financial information requirements stipulated in the Basel Accords. Most of these changes resulted in improvements in the disclosure of financial information due to the reformulation of accounting rules for entries and reporting. These reformulations were designed to improve the informational quality of statements so that they accurately represent the true performance of the bank.

The Sarbanes Oxley Act (2002), introduced in response to a series of corporate scandals in the US, requires organisations, in particular banks, to identify, assess, and test the effectiveness of their key management controls and monitor the business to ensure greater accountability, transparency, and compliance with laws and regulations (Merchant and Van der Stede, 2007). Such changes demand the use of stringent management systems in banks with implications for the adoption of new types of management procedures, including the introduction of new performance measures.

3.5.2 *Mimetic pressures*

DiMaggio and Powell (1983) argue that in an uncertain environment, organisations will imitate others in determining appropriate behaviour. Adapting operational or decision-making systems to imitate the systems used by industry leaders is seen as a means of reducing uncertainty and risk, and enhancing legitimacy (Greve, 2000; DiMaggio and Powell, 1983). For instance, banks that lack the ability to implement and utilise their own PMSs tend to copy publicly accredited best practices from other successful banks, or from manufacturing organisations (O'Neill et al., 1998; Fligstein, 1985). This tendency of modelling the practices of successful organisations stems from a desire to gain legitimacy from their operating environment, with larger and better performing banks serving as a strong role model for other banking institutions (McKendrick, 1995). Moreover, when macro-level factors require banks to change their PMSs, in certain situations, banks merely adopt best practices in the industry in order to signal to stakeholders their intention to improve efficiency.

Anecdotal evidence also suggests that mimetic behaviour occurs through a number of formal and informal avenues. For example, by recruiting professional and well-trained employees from other banks, and using them to develop similar systems to the ones they used in the past.

3.5.3 *Normative pressures*

According to DiMaggio and Powell (1991), normative pressure stems primarily from pressures from professionals. They describe professionalism as the collective struggle of members of an occupation, with shared educational and professional experience, and infrastructure that establishes norms of behaviour that are reflected in the management of its institutions (DiMaggio and Powell, 1991, p. 152). In the banking sector, credit rating agencies, bankers' professional associations, and banks' training institutions reinforce normative expectations and impose standards, rules, and values on banks. Normative pressures can be exerted by professionals, top management, and the organisational culture prevailing in a bank.

Professionals

DiMaggio and Powell (1983) identify professionals as having the most dominant influence on organisational practices. Professional networks such as associations of accountants are known as an important source of isomorphism (Scapens, 1994; DiMaggio and Powell, 1991). For instance, in researching management control practices, Scapens (1994, p. 317) regarded the influence of managers as an important factor in the adoption of new management practices. In particular, Hussain and Hoque (2002, p. 167) acknowledge that "the experience of professionals such as managers may also influence the design and use of a performance measurement system". Thus, professionals in a banking context, including bankers associations and bankers' training institutions such as the Institute of International Bankers and the World Bank's Economic Development Institute, could have a direct or an indirect influence on the PMSs that are used within banks.

Top management

The role of top management and the nature and level of power which they possess perform an important role in negotiating change in management accounting systems within organisations (Kaplan and Norton, 2001). Modell (2007) claims that top management plays a crucial role in successfully introducing changes to management practices. They maintain that top management needs to develop a commitment to change by creating a vision for change, by a readiness to change and by describing the expected outcomes of the change and developing support by clearly addressing the dynamics of the proposed management accounting system change. Similarly, Francis (2002) argues that top management needs to bring into existence the new reality within which employees frame the changes within the management accounting system. Such perspectives recognise that top management needs to use power constructively in encouraging commitment and preparing employees for the challenges inherent in the change process. Conversely, the misuse of power can result in inhibiting change with disastrous consequences for the organisation (Kasurinen, 2002).

Granlund and Lukka (1998) and Scott (1987) argue that top management often creates cultural forms consistent with their own aims and beliefs. These, in turn, influence organisational practices and systems, including PMSs. The existing literature suggests that board members and chief financial officers can influence changes in PMSs. For instance, Cobb et al. (1995) explicitly state that such individuals are generally considered as significant change agents. Cobb et al.

(1995) also found top management playing a dual role in a bank's change process; on the one hand, top management was the catalyst which initiated management accounting change processes and, on the other hand, their leadership ability was found to be necessary to overcome barriers. This implies that top management plays a crucial role in PMS change.

Corporate culture

Corporate culture refers to the combined beliefs, values, ethics, procedures, and atmosphere of an organisation (Pettigrew, 1979). Corporate culture can influence the attitudes of employees about work practices, their commitment, respect for managers, and attitudes towards providing service to customers. Further, the tradition of a particular industry could strongly affect the culture of an organisation (Pettigrew, 1979). For example, banks and bankers have a risk-averse nature, and therefore they often choose systems and procedures which minimise overall organisational risk. Hence, the manner in which a bank is managed is likely to be influenced by the beliefs, attitudes, and behaviour of employees towards adopting and using a particular procedure and system. If employees resist a particular change due to the corporate culture prevailing in the bank, it may lead to conflict, negotiation, and/or compromise.

The Basel Committee on Banking Supervision has also strongly emphasised that a bank's framework for managing operational risk must include the bank's appetite and tolerance for operational risk. The extent to which this is done is mainly contingent on a bank's corporate culture (Basel Committee on Banking Supervision, 2004, p. 167). Corporate culture can therefore be regarded as a factor that influences organisational systems in general, and PMSs in particular.

3.6 Strategic responses to change efforts

There is ample evidence in the literature to suggest that organisations do not always passively conform to changes, and that their response to change varies. Drawing on institutional theory and the resource dependence perspective,[8] Oliver (1991) identified different strategic responses and tactics which organisations use in response to institutional pressures for change. More specifically, Oliver (1991) proposed a typology of strategic responses to institutional pressures which shows that strategic responses to institutional pressures vary with the degree of resistance exerted by the organisation (Table 3.1).

As shown in Table 3.1, at times, banks would passively respond (i.e., an acquiescence strategy) to change efforts, and such response may take different forms varying from unconscious, habit-like adherence to rules or values, to conscious compliance to norms, values, or institutional requirements (Oliver, 1991, p. 152). Such acquiescence is a strategic response that concurs with the idea of mimetic isomorphism. For example, most small local/domestic banks are likely to imitate the practices of major banks and foreign banks when there is pressure to introduce change.

Table 3.1 A continuum of strategic responses to institutional pressures

	Strategies	*Tactics*	*Examples*
Low	**Acquiescence**	Habit	Following invisible, taken-
		Imitate	for-granted norms
		Comply	Mimicking institutional models
			Obeying rules and accepting norms
	Compromise	Balance	Balancing the expectations of
		Pacify	multiple constituents
		Bargain	Placating and accommodating
			institutional elements
Level of active			Negotiating with institutional
resistance to			stakeholders
institutional	**Avoid**	Conceal	Disguising nonconformity
pressures		Buffer	Loosening institutional
		Escape	attachments
			Changing goals, activities, or
			domains
	Defy	Dismiss	Ignoring explicit norms and values
		Challenge	Contesting rules and requirements
		Attack	Assaulting the sources of
High			institutional pressure
	Manipulate	Co-opt	Importing influential constituents
		Influence	Shaping values and criteria
		Control	Dominating institutional
			constituents and processes

Source: Oliver (1991, p. 152)

Alternatively, banks may take more active responses to institutional pressures (i.e., a compromise strategy). Where inconsistencies exist between institutional expectations and the objectives of the bank, banks are likely to apply balancing tactics (i.e., attempt to achieve parity among or between multiple stakeholders and internal interests), or pacifying (i.e., monitoring a minor level of resistance to institutional pressure) or bargaining tactics (Oliver, 1991, p. 153). Such responses are likely to arise particularly in relation to banks operating internationally. Bank branches located overseas might face a situation where the host banking sector's objectives are in dissonance with the organisational objective of the bank. For example, risk management practices, central bank capital adequacy and liquidity requirements, and prudential regulations vary from country to country.

In some situations, banks may use an "avoidance" strategy in order to preclude the necessity of conformity (Oliver, 1991, p. 154). To achieve this purpose, they may use a number of tactics. For instance, concealment tactics which involve disguising nonconformity behind a façade of acquiescence, or buffering tactics which involve attempts to reduce the extent to which it is externally inspected, scrutinised, or evaluated by partially detaching or decoupling its technical activities from external contact (Scott, 1987; Pfeffer and Salancik, 1978). A more dramatic avoidance response is "escape", where a bank decides to exit the domain within which pressure is exerted, or significantly alter its own goals, activities, or domain to avoid the necessity of conformity altogether (Oliver, 1991). The banking literature provides evidence of banks operating overseas which have exited (escaped) or buffered themselves from the host banking sector due to an uncertain economic, financial, and political environment. For example, in the late 1990s the Bank of America, J.P. Morgan, and the Credit Agricole Indosuez banks pulled out of their operations in East Asian countries (Fuller, 1999).

Alternatively, a bank could ignore institutional rules and values which challenge the existing rules and requirements (i.e., a defiance strategy). The most aggressive defiance tactic is attacking the institutional pressures and expectations (Oliver, 1991, p. 156). Rather than partially refusing to follow the newly recommended procedures (i.e., the avoidance strategy), banks may decide to actively challenge the proposed procedures (i.e., the defiance strategy). Further, a bank could even focus on changing the content of the expectations themselves, or the sources that seek to express or reinforce them (i.e., a manipulation strategy). As a tactic, a bank may choose to co-opt the source of the pressure or direct more general influence tactics towards institutionalised values and beliefs, and the criteria of acceptable practices or performance. Banks could also apply controlling tactics whereby they would exert efforts to establish power and dominance over those that are applying pressure on the banks (Oliver, 1991, p. 157). For example, large banks tend to create cartels to lobby regulatory authorities to adopt certain practices that fit their needs.

Oliver's (1991) typology provides an appropriate conceptual basis for exploring the diversity in the strategic responses of a bank to the institutional pressures to change their PMS. In addition to classifying strategic responses, Oliver (1991, p. 160) hypothesised conditions where different strategic responses would be most likely. She identified five factors (namely, Cause, Constituents, Contents, Control, and Context), which relate to the willingness and ability of organisations to conform to institutional pressures, and hence may be regarded as antecedents of strategic responses (see Table 3.2). "Cause" refers to the basic question of why the organisation is being pressured to conform to the institutional rules or expectations. For example, in countries where the banking sector is subject to reform, such reforms may be seen as the underlying cause of institutional pressure. Further,

Table 3.2 Antecedents of strategic responses

Institutional factor	Research question
Cause	Why is the organisation being pressured to conform to institutional rules or expectations?
Constituents	Who is exerting institutional pressure on the organisation?
Content	To what norms or requirements is the organisation pressured to conform?
Control	How or by what means are the institutional pressures being exerted?
Context	What is the environmental context within which institutional pressures are being exerted?

Source: Oliver (1991, p. 160)

the introduction of Basel Accords I and II in 1988 and 2003/04 respectively was a major factor in generating pressure on central banks to improve banking institutions' capital requirements, supervision, and market discipline.

Moreover, a central factor in predicting the nature of strategic responses is the institutional "constituents". In Oliver's (1991) terminology, they are the ones who exert institutional pressures. In the context of banks, these include the government, the central bank, professionals, borrowers, depositors, and international financial institutions such as the IMF and the World Bank. Oliver (1991, p. 162) hypothesised that when there are more constituents and the less the organisation is dependent on them, the greater the likelihood of organisational resistance to institutional pressures. Furthermore, the easiest way for an organisation to cope with the multiple demands of its institutional constituents is to comply with the demands of those institutions that they depend on most (i.e., the central bank in case of the banking sector). For example, developing countries are under pressure from the IMF and the World Bank to implement the Basel Accords and international regulatory benchmarks even though they are voluntary. Countries that do not implement such regulations face sanctions, such as termination of lending facilities from international financial institutions like the World Bank, IMF, Asian Development Bank, and KFW Development Bank (Kreditanstalt Für Wiederaufbau – German Development Bank). Further, bank branches from developing countries are allowed to operate in developed countries only if their home country central bank complies with the Basel Standards (Hilbers et al., 2000).

The "content" of institutional pressure is another factor that can be used to predict organisational responses. Organisations are likely to resist institutional pressures when they are inconsistent with organisational goals and/or when conformity to institutional pressures leads to a loss in organisational decision-making freedom (Oliver, 1991, p. 164). In other words, organisations selectively comply with those pressures that are in line with their strategy and that do not threaten their independence. For example, if a government demands a public bank (in which the government is the main shareholder) to invest in a particular segment of the industry/economy, contrary to the policy of the bank, the bank is likely to use some strategy to resist the change. "Control" is another factor used to predict organisational responses. For instance, the lower the degree of legal coercion or enforcement, the greater the likelihood of organisational resistance to institutional pressures (Oliver, 1991, p. 167). This implies that weak enforcement by the government of certain legislations/regulations on the banking sector would delineate the effectiveness of the legislative change.

Finally, the environmental "context" can also predict the likelihood of organisational resistance. Organisations are more likely to resist institutional pressures when the level of uncertainty and the degree of interconnectedness in their environments are low. This is consistent with the idea of institutional isomorphic change as related to field level factors. In order to cope with environment uncertainty, organisations look for templates (archetypes) of successful organisations from their environment (Greenwood and Hinings, 1996, p. 1026). For instance, banks might mimic other banks with high profitability and stability, thereby conforming to institutional pressures.

3.7 An analytical framework to examine change

This chapter draws on theoretical constructs from DiMaggio and Powell (1983) and Oliver (1991) to develop an analytical framework. The proposed framework, depicted in Figure 3.1, shows that the functioning of banks is subject to the influence of various macro-level factors (i.e., economic, technological, socio-cultural, and political), and the resulting institutional pressures could take various forms (i.e., coercive, mimetic, and normative). These pressures could lead to the introduction of changes to control systems including PMSs. While banks may consider introducing certain changes to their PMSs because of these pressures, the change efforts may also be subject to direct pressure from certain powerful elements in the macro-level environment. Such influences may be exerted using informal avenues, and the nature and the extent of the recommended change could be the result of both formal (i.e., coercive, mimetic, and normative pressures) and informal pressures (the direct influence of macro-level elements) showed by a dotted link in Figure 3.1. The framework also acknowledges that banks' response to change efforts could vary between passive responses (i.e., acquiescence) to active responses (i.e., manipulation), depending on the nature and intensity of the pressures to change.

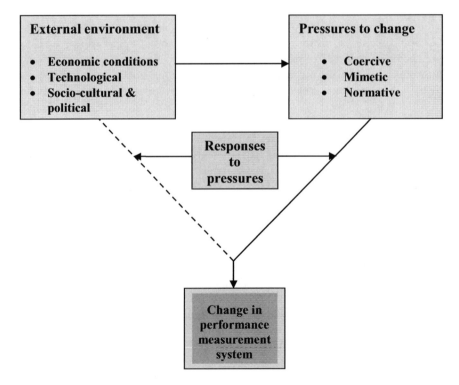

Figure 3.1 Analytical framework for performance measurement system changes

3.8 Summary

The purpose of this chapter was to develop an analytical framework to examine changes in the PMS of the case organisation. The framework uses concepts from institutional theory, more specifically DiMaggio and Powell's (1983) notion of institutional pressures, to offer a broader explanation as to what influences banks to change their performance measurement practices. The framework also used insights from Oliver's (1991) typology of strategic responses to institutional pressures to change. These theoretical constructs were chosen for their ability to provide a comprehensive explanation of the PMS change phenomenon. The framework developed in this chapter will be used to analyse the changes in the PMS of the bank investigated in this research, and address the following research questions: (i) What factors influenced the changes in the PMS of the bank investigated? and (ii) How did the bank respond to the factors driving change in the performance measurement system?

Notes

1 Suchman (1995) segregated legitimacy into three groups: pragmatic legitimacy, moral legitimacy, and cognitive legitimacy. He asserts that all types of legitimacy involve "a generalized perception that organisational activities are desirable, proper and appropriate with certain socially constructed systems of values, norms, beliefs and definitions" (p. 577).
2 Institutions are composed of "cultural-cognitive, normative, and regulative elements that together with associated activities and resources provide stability and meaning to social life" (Scott, 2001, p. 48).
3 To explain this notion, DiMaggio and Powell (1983) introduced the concept of organisational fields to analyse the context of an organisation which includes closely related suppliers, customers, regulators, competitors, or other important inter-organisational links which are important determinants of institutional pressures.
4 Legitimacy is a "generalized perception or assumption that the actions of an entity are desirable, proper, or appropriate within some socially constructed system of norms, values, beliefs, and definitions" (Suchman, 1995, p. 574). Legitimacy theory posits that businesses are bound by the social contract in which the organisations agree to perform various socially desired actions in return for approval of its objectives and other rewards, and this ultimately guarantees its continued existence (Dowling and Pfeffer, 1975).
5 An explanation of these responses is provided in Section 3.6.
6 See for details Operational Risk Management, and Risk Management in the New Regulatory Environment (Basel Committee on Banking Supervision, 1998).
7 As described in Chapter 1, the CAMELS framework involves analysis of specific groups of performance measures, namely Capital adequacy, Assets quality, Management, Earning quality, Liquidity, and Sensitivity (market risk). The CAELS framework involves analysis of four groups of performance measures, namely Capital adequacy, Assets quality, Earning quality, Liquidity, and Sensitivity.
8 The resource dependence perspective views an organisational environment as a bundle of resources which an organisation seeks to mobilise to reach its goals. In doing so, it exercises active choice of behaviour (Oliver, 1991, p. 147).

4 Research method

4.1 Introduction

The purpose of this chapter is to describe the research method used in this research. The research utilises a qualitative research approach, in particular the case research method. The data were collected from the case organisation, for the period 1997–2017, using multiple data sources including a questionnaire, semi-structured interviews, and relevant internal and external documents. The data was used to address the following questions: (i) How did the performance measurement system in a bank operating in Pakistan change over the last decade? (ii) What factors influenced the changes? and (iii) How did the bank respond to the factors driving change in the performance measurement system?

The remainder of the chapter is divided into eight sections. A brief discussion of the research strategy is provided in Section 4.2. The approach used to select the case organisation and the participants of the research is then described in Sections 4.3 and 4.4 respectively. Section 4.5 provides a detailed description of the method used to collect data, including the construction of the questions and the administration of the questionnaire and interviews. Section 4.6 provides an overview of the data analysis approach. Section 4.7 discusses the validity and reliability issues covering the research. Finally, a summary of the chapter is provided in Section 4.8.

4.2 Research strategy

As outlined earlier in the book, the purpose of this research is to understand the changes in the performance measurement system (PMS) of banks by exploring the factors that influence them to change performance measurement practices and examining the bank's consequential responses to such pressures. The view taken in this research is that performance measurement is not a static phenomenon but, rather, it adapts and changes in response to the pressures generated in the organisational environment. Such a view suggests the importance of researching the PMS change phenomenon in its organisational context or natural setting. Qualitative research methods are deemed appropriate as they enable researchers to research social phenomena in their natural setting (Patton, 2002). According to Murray (2003), "Qualitative research is multi-method in focus, involving an interpretive, naturalistic approach to its subject matter" (pp. 1–2). Unlike quantitative research, which seeks causal determination, prediction, and generalisation of findings, qualitative research seeks illumination, understanding, and extrapolation to similar situations (Hopper and Powell, 1985). Further, this particular research method entails the involvement of the researcher in exploring and describing the behaviour of people and events (Murray, 2003). There are several advantages to adopting qualitative research. For instance, Das (1983) suggests that in qualitative research, the researcher is involved with the phenomenon of research to uncover perceptions, attitudes, and behaviours of the participants. Human experience is crucial in conducting qualitative research, either through the participants' point of view or through the researcher's interpretation (Ryan et al., 2002, p. 147; Creswell, 1994), or both.

The motivation to use qualitative research for this research comes from the consideration that control systems such as PMSs are "socio-economic" phenomenon influenced by a variety of macro-level environments (e.g., economic and political conditions, socio-cultural factors, and technological innovations) and institutional influences (e.g., coercive, mimetic, and normative). The influence of these environments and responses to such influences could be analysed more appropriately while researching them in their natural context using multiple data sources from inside and outside the organisation being investigated. Further, qualitative research, in particular the case research method, is considered appropriate as it enables an in-depth examination of the research phenomenon.

4.2.1 Case study method

In investigating the factors that influenced the case organisation to change its PMS and the consequential responses to such pressures, the case study method enables the researcher to enter the site and ascertain the changes in the PMS as understood by the participants of the research. Yin (2002) defines a case study as "an empirical inquiry that investigates a contemporary phenomenon within its real life context, especially when the boundaries between phenomena and context are not clearly evident; and in which multiple sources of evidence is used" (p. 13). In a case study, the researcher investigates multiple aspects of a particular case through extensive data that often comes in a qualitative form (Das, 1983). Yin (2002) notes that the inquiry copes with situations in which there are many more variables of interest than data points, and relies on multiple sources of evidence. In this research, individual managers and different stakeholders of the bank are allowed a voice to build a rich understanding of the research phenomenon. This method allows the researcher to examine the participants' views within the specific and unique institutional context of the banking sector in Pakistan.

Yin (2002) suggests that case studies may have multiple purposes: explanatory, exploratory, and descriptive. In an explanatory case study, generally, theories are used in order to provide an understanding and explanation of the specific case. Sometimes when a theory cannot provide sufficient explanation of the phenomenon under investigation, the researcher will turn to modify an existing theory, or to develop a new theory to extend an explanation of the case (Yin, 2002). The exploratory case study method is used to explore a given phenomenon in order to address the "what" questions (Neuman, 2004), and the fieldwork and data collection is undertaken prior to defining the research questions. Researchers use the descriptive case study method to address "how" and "who" questions. The descriptive case study is often used to describe contemporary systems and practices, possibly with a view to determining best practice (Yin, 2002). This research aims to describe a PMS change in a bank in Pakistan and provide explanations.

A case study either includes a single case or multiple cases depending on the aim of the research. According to Yin (1994), a single case study is preferred when it represents a critical case and because it enables the researcher to provide a deeper understanding of the complexity and uniqueness of a research issue. The multiple case study method is often used when there is need for replication. Each case either predicts similar results or produces contrasting results, with the analysis primarily concerned with comparisons between the cases (Yin, 1994). Since the aim of this research was to examine issues in relation to one particular bank rather than to compare and contrast the findings between cases, the single case study method was preferred.

4.3 Selection of the case organisation

The selection of a suitable case was primarily based on what could be learned in line with the purpose of the research (Yin, 1994). According to Yin (1994), there is a potential risk in conducting case studies when a case may turn out not to be the case it was thought to be at the beginning. Therefore, the case organisation must be selected carefully to prevent misrepresentations in relation to understanding, describing, and explaining the data that will be collected. Further, the potential for gaining access to the organisation, having sufficient resources while in the field, and possibilities for unanticipated events, such as the resignation of a participant during the data collection period, must be considered prior to entering the research field. Further, the case should be selected based on the opportunities it offers to provide new insights and to advance our knowledge of the field of research (Young and Selto, 1993). Yin (1993) suggests that researchers should carefully select case organisations, and carefully examine the choices available for data sources in order to increase the validity and reliability of the research. Following the above guidance, well-structured criteria were established for identifying and selecting the case organisation and the potential participants. The following criteria were used in this research to select the case organisation:

i   The banking sector (research field) must be located in an emerging economy and the sector must have undergone change prior to or during the period under investigation;

ii   The bank must have been in business for at least one decade, be well diversified in its operational activities, and have formally implemented management
accounting systems (including the PMS);

iii The bank must have changed its PMS during the last two decades (i.e., prior
to 2017) and the new PMS must have been in use for at least five years; and

iv   The researcher must have access to the information needed for the research.

Pakistan's banking sector was chosen because of the many regulatory and institutional changes experienced during the period from 1997 to 2017 as a result
of the World Bank and the IMF's assisted financial sector reforms.[1] The financial sector reforms in 1997 had profound implications for the banking sector in
Pakistan, including the case organisation. These reforms led to organisational
restructuring, changes in strategy, and eventually changes in the PMS of the case
organisation. Accordingly, the year 1997 was chosen as a starting point to explore
and examine changes in the PMS in the case organisation.

Five potential banks from Pakistan's banking sector were identified through
internet searches, publicly available information, and the prior knowledge of the
researcher and his personal contacts. One of the largest state-owned banks was
identified as its management had shown their willingness to participate in the
research. The management of the other four banks, which were recently privatised, had shown reluctance in providing documents of interest and participating
in interviews. On request by the selected bank, the name of the bank has been
changed (to FUB) and some information disguised so as to not reveal the identity
of the bank or the participants.

FUB was contacted to verify whether they met the criteria set for the selection
of the case organisation. The bank was approached through a member of the
Management Committee.[2] This member was the head of the human resource
group of FUB (hereafter "organisation contact"). He was contacted via telephone by the researcher and given detailed information concerning all aspects
of the research. During the telephone conversation the identity and credentials
of the researcher and the purpose of the research were provided. After consulta-
tion with the bank's President, the organisation contact informed the researcher
of the bank's willingness to participate in the research. The organisation contact
also indicated that the findings would be useful in improving FUB's performance
measurement practices. Upon the request of the researcher, the organisation contact provided primary information such as annual reports and details regarding
FUB's operations and management structure. This information was used to gain
a background understanding of FUB.

4.3.1 The case bank (FUB)

FUB has been operating in Pakistan over the last six decades and has been the
banker of the government and trustee of public funds. It has diversified its business portfolio and is currently a major player in the debt equity market, corporate investment banking, retail and consumer banking, agricultural financing, and

treasury services in the country. The bank has built an extensive branch network, with over 1,550 branches in Pakistan, and in major international business centres. It has agency arrangements with more than 3,000 correspondent banks world-wide. In 1997, in order to redefine its role from a public sector organisation into a modern commercial bank, a number of initiatives were undertaken, in terms of institutional restructuring, changes in the field structure, policies and procedures, and control systems. The emphasis of these changes was on corporate govern-ance and performance measurement, the adoption of capital adequacy stand-ards under the Basel II framework, and up-grading the information technology infrastructure.

Following the financial sector reforms in 1997, FUB could no longer rely solely on traditional ways to manage and control its business. Rather, the bank had to employ a more proactive market-based approach, focusing on higher profit margins, customer-oriented businesses, and sophisticated banking tech-nologies in order to compete with the foreign and newly formed private banks. In particular, the structural and regulatory changes had significant implications for FUB's PMS, specifically in regard to the selection of performance measures for key business operations and management activities. The significant changes experienced in FUB provided an interesting research setting to examine the fac-tors that influenced changes in PMSs and the responses to such factors.

4.4 Selection of the participants

Careful selection of respondents is critical in case studies as interviews are the main source of data and such data is critical for the case findings (McKinnon, 1988, p. 51). To qualify for this research, prospective participants were required: (i) to be involved in the design, implementation, and/or use of PMSs within FUB; (ii) to have completed at least five years' service with the bank just prior to 2007; and (iii) to be willing to participate in the research voluntarily. The organi-sational contact's assistance was sought to identify managers from different hier-archical levels who met the above criteria. The involvement of the organisation contact in the process of identifying potential participants was seen as a means of gaining their support once they had agreed to participate in the research (Young and Selto, 1993).

Twelve individuals were deemed to be the most suitable to participate in this research due to their knowledge of the changes experienced by FUB, includ-ing the PMS.[3] The participants represented both senior (business group heads), and middle and lower management levels (regional and branch managers), and a number of functional areas.[4] The selection of participants from different func-tional areas and hierarchical levels was intended to obtain different perspectives of the same phenomenon and also to improve the validity and reliability of the research (Yin, 2001). Among the respondents, eight were from the corporate office and four were from regional offices and branches. With the exception of one participant, the interviewees had at least eight years' experience working at FUB with four of them having joined the bank prior to 1997. Immediately after obtaining contact details of the potential participants of the research, initial contact was made with each potential participant by phone in an attempt to ascertain their interest in the research and to introduce the researcher. During this phone call, the aim of the research and the participation requirements were explained to them. All participants agreed to participate in the research. Table 4.1 summarises the profile of the participants.

After obtaining ethics approval from the University to undertake this research, in November 2007 an information letter was sent through the organisation contact to each participant formally inviting them to participate in this research. The organisation contact and participants were assured of the confidentiality of the data gathered from them. Participants were also informed that they would receive a summary report of the findings of the research after the data analysis was completed using a format that would protect the confidentiality of the participants of the research.

Table 4.1 Profile of the research participants

Participant*	Area of responsibility	Years' experience in banking	Years' experience with FUB	Approx. length of interview (minutes)
Business Group Head 1	Corporate Office	28	9	80
Business Group Head 2	Corporate Office	25	9	75
Business Group Head 3	Corporate Office	26	10	85
Business Group Head 4	Corporate Office	22	5	95
Business Group Head 5	Corporate Office	17	8	75
Business Group Head 6	Corporate Office	30	30	80
Business Group Head 7	Corporate Office	25	25	70
Business Group Head 8	Corporate Office	21	9	65
Regional Manager 1	Regional Office	29	9	70
Regional Manager 2	Regional Office	31	31	80
Branch Manager 1	Branch	28	12	90
Branch Manager 2	Branch	16	10	80

*All participants were male with the exception of Business Group Head 8.
NB: A meeting was also held with the bank President. The meeting with the bank President was not structured according to the interview guide; however it provided a useful insight into his views concerning the changes introduced in FUB.

4.5 Data collection process

Multiple data sources were used to address the research questions in the book. According to Yin (1994), the use of multiple sources of information within a single case research enables data triangulation. Yin (1994) further argues that such an approach allows the researcher to explain a range of issues related to the phenomena under research. The data sources in this research include: (i) documents of interest (both internal and external); (ii) the administration of a questionnaire to the participants of the research; and (iii) semi-structured interviews. The use of multiple sources of data was also expected to improve the validity and reliability of the research (McKinnon, 1988). The following subsections describe the data sources used in the research in more detail.

4.5.1 Documents

According to Yin (1994), documents have an important part in data collection by providing access to valuable official information in case studies. Yin (1994) further argues that documents are important as a data source in a case research, because they not only provide data which could be used to validate the responses of the participants, but also generate new insights and inferences which can lead to new lines of inquiry (Yin, 1994, p. 84). However, care must be taken in interpreting documents, since they are often prepared for another purpose and a different audience than that of the case research. One strength of using documents as a source of evidence is that they contain exact names, references, and details of events, and they entail a broad coverage over a long time span, of many events, and many settings. However, there are also certain weaknesses in relation to the use of documentary evidence which must be noted. Specifically, the accessibility to certain documents may be low, or access may be deliberately blocked. There may also be bias in interpreting documents when the data collected is incomplete. Further, misinterpretations of the data by the author may pose significant threats to the validity of the research findings (Yin, 1994).

To understand the macro-level and institutional context, and also to gain insights into the organisation's perspective, internal and external documents were used in this research. These documents were collected for the period from 1997 to 2017. The documents utilised were mainly internal records, and included FUB's performance measurement reports, corporate plans, training strategy, and compliance manual. Notes were also taken from the minutes of relevant Management Committee meetings. Furthermore, evidence available from other documentary records, such as published annual reports from 1995 onwards, were collected and reviewed. The review of annual reports was expected to provide an understanding of the nature of changes within the bank and various management initiatives. Annual reports were also reviewed to better understand the events that took place outside the bank during the period under investigation. In addition, relevant media reports were also collected and reviewed to develop a better understanding of external impressions about FUB, the changes that had taken place in the industry in the previous decade, and to obtain an external perspective on the changes within FUB. Information gathered from these documents was also useful in focusing the discussions in the interviews and in clarifying any obscurities.

The central bank in Pakistan (the regulators) was also visited prior to the interviews to collect annual reports, regulatory and banking policies, and information about Pakistan's banking sector for the period under investigation. A meeting was also held with each of the heads of the State Bank's "Audit and Compliance" and "Banking Policy and Regulations" departments to capture the regulators' view of the changes in the banking sector. The relevant comments provided by the heads of these two departments were noted to validate interviewees' responses and to improve the validity and reliability of the research (McKinnon, 1988). In addition, speeches of the Governor of the State Bank of Pakistan highlighting changes within Pakistan's banking sector were collected from the Bank's publication department, while pertinent IMF technical notes and other public documents on the condition of the banking system in Pakistan were gathered to develop a better understanding of the changes that occurred in the industry prior to and after the 1997 financial sector reforms. These documents provided an insight into the industry-specific factors affecting FUB, and were also used to focus the discussion in the interviews.

4.5.2 *Questionnaire*

A questionnaire was designed to supplement the interviews (Dillman, 1999) and provide a preliminary insight into FUB's PMS and the views of participants. The questions were developed from relevant literature on performance measurement systems (e.g., Tsamenyi et al., 2006; Almqvist and Skoog, 2006; Chenhall, 2003; Hussain and Hoque, 2002; Soin et al., 2002; Helliar et al., 2002; Waggoner et al., 1999; Greenwood and Hinings, 1996; Neely et al., 1995; Cobb et al., 1995; Innes and Mitchell, 1990; Khandwalla, 1977).

The questionnaire was divided into four broad questions with each containing a range of closed-ended responses. Respondents were required to indicate the extent to which: (i) the PMS was used to achieve specific objectives both at the present point in time and prior to 1997; (ii) specific performance measures were used both at the present point in time and prior to 1997; (iii) specific factors impacted on PMS change over the ten-year period; and (iv) specific factors were important in facilitating the successful implementation of new PMSs. Respondents were required to indicate their responses using a 5-point Likert scale with anchors of "Not at all" and "To a great extent".

4.5.3 *Semi-structured interviews*

There are three types of interviews: structured, semi-structured, and unstructured. Structured interviews follow a set sequence of questions. Unstructured interviews do not follow a particular sequence and comprise an open discussion about a particular issue. Semi-structured interviews, in comparison to the above, allow the researcher the freedom to alter the sequence of questions. In semi-structured interviews the flow of discussions can be altered depending on the interviewee's responses and the researcher's initiative, and the researcher can exercise the freedom to include unexpected questions which can bring in unknown and insightful information. Considering these strengths, the semi-structured interview method was preferred to collect the data to address the research questions of this research. Semi-structured interviews also provided the opportunity to ask probing questions which offered the researcher deeper insights into the PMS change phenomenon being investigated.

Following the literature review, an interview guide was developed to facilitate the interviews. The interview guide (see Appendix) contained eighteen open-ended questions. Using Dillard and Reilly's (1988) notion for dividing the interview into sections, the interview guide was divided into three sections with an initial few questions designed to establish rapport and make the respondents feel comfortable. The middle section of the interview guide dealt with the reasons and rationale for changing the PMS pre- and post-1997, the nature and types of changes, any resistance by staff, and the nature of such resistance and the steps taken to manage it. The latter part of the guide dealt more with what the respondents thought about the entire process of change.

The questions were designed to be short, simple, and comprehensible, avoiding ambiguous, vague, and presumptuous wording (Yin, 1994). Further, considerable attention was paid to determine the sequence of the questions in order to make it easy for respondents to understand the flow of questions. The questions were framed using simple and clear language which could be easily understood by the respondents, who came from different departments and backgrounds within FUB. The use of any technical and ambiguous terms was avoided so that the respondent felt relaxed and comfortable to talk about issues.

In early 2017 the organisation contact and participants willing to participate in the research were sent a copy of the questionnaire and the interview guide. Subsequently, all participants of the research were contacted individually by phone. During this contact, the purpose of the research was again explained and the participants were informed that their participation was very important for the success of the research and that any information they would provide would be kept confidential. They were informed that in general, thirty–thirty-five minutes were required from participants to complete the questionnaire and that interviews would last approximately between seventy-five–ninety minutes. To accommodate the language preference of the participants involved in this research, participants were asked if a translated version (in Urdu, Pakistan's national language) of the questionnaire and interview guide was required. As the official language of Pakistan's banking sector is English, all participants expressed their comfort in using English in this process. This approach helped the researcher to avoid potential threats to the validity of interview responses stemming from problems of translation.

A meeting with the participants of the research was held at the corporate office of FUB. The purpose of this meeting was to establish rapport between each respondent and the researcher and to clarify the interviewer's role as well as the respondent's role. At the end of this meeting, an interview schedule was developed. The participants were again provided with a copy of the questionnaire and interview guide and they were informed that the questionnaire could be sent to the organisation contact prior to the interview in a sealed envelope provided by the researcher. The interview time and place was confirmed with each of the participants two days before the scheduled time. The questionnaire was collected before the interview and scanned to obtain a profile of the participant. At the beginning of the interview, each participant was again reminded of the objective and scope of the research. All the interviews were tape recorded with prior permission from the participants. Each interview was about one to one-and-a-half hours' duration.

As indicated earlier, prior to the interviews, the minutes of the Management Committee and the Board of Directors' meetings, and internal memoranda and circulars concerning performance measurement for the period from 1997 to 2017, were carefully reviewed to identify information relevant to this research. Further, documents and the press interviews of the bank's President provided a useful basis to direct the attention of interviewees to the critical events impacting the change initiatives undertaken after 1997, including changes in organisational structure, strategy, and PMS. As part of the triangulation method, interviewees were asked to provide examples of reports and documents they used (Yin, 1994). Moreover, their responses were compared with the documents obtained from them (McKinnon, 1988). Comparison of the interviewees' responses with the documentary evidence suggested that the interviewees had not portrayed themselves in a way that would invalidate the interpretations drawn from their responses. Towards the end of each interview, time was provided for open and informal discussion to extract information which participants might otherwise have been reluctant to provide during the formal interviews. These informal discussions allowed the researcher to probe deeper into the issues relevant to the research.

4.6 Data coding and analysis

The recorded interviews were transcribed verbatim prior to commencing data coding and analysis. Data was coded and analysed using the qualitative data program Nvivo and the methods recommended by Eisenhardt (1989). This approach adopts an iterative process involving data validation and reduction, data display and identification of emerging themes, and interpreting data and conclusion drawing in terms of the analytical framework of the research. Prior to the beginning of the coding, a set of coding rules was established. These coding rules are shown in Table 4.2.

Stage one of the coding process began by loading all the transcripts into Nvivo. Then all interviews were coded, to classify the data into categories, by linking passages in the interview document using two coding schemas reflecting either (i) a reason for change, mechanism or process for change and (ii) a reaction or

Table 4.2 Rules for the coding process

Step	Rules
1	Primary idea which is central to the research is to be coded as a node.
2	The newly created nodes are to be renamed and truncated to one–two words or as precisely and generically as possible.
3	The nodes are then tested for uniqueness. The context of the repeated nodes is to be combined and then the repeated nodes are to be deleted.
4	If a node spans more than two meanings, then it is to be broken up into two.
5	Steps 2–4 are to be repeated till such time that no further changes can be done.
6	The nodes are then to be grouped together into main codes based on some similarity between them.
7	Repeat step 6 till such time that no nodes are left.
8	Repeat step 7 till such time that no further groups can be formed.

resistance to change. The first schema was used to investigate factors that influenced changes, the second schema was used to analyse responses to the pressures to change.

Stage two consisted of going through steps 2–5 of the coding rules outlined in Table 4.2. Every interview was coded based on the questions that were used in the interview guide. Thereafter, the codes were categorised into nodes. The nodes were derived from the key questions that were asked during the interviews. Thus, the nodes were not developed from the participant's own choice of vocabulary. For example, one interviewee said:

> the change in banking landscape, until eight years ago all commercial banks in Pakistan whether they were nationalized commercial banks like [. . .] private Pakistani banks or foreign banks like [. . .] were all focusing on either large corporate entities and public sector companies, or on buying treasury bills, because interest rates were very high and there was a large arbitrage in simply taking deposits and investing in treasury bills and most of the banks were doing that not only in the treasury bills but also in National Saving Scheme of Government of Pakistan. The reason the interest rates were high was in part because of the weakness of the rupee and in part because of the very high borrowing requirements implemented by the government.
>
> . . . the bank did not want to access the market sectors in Pakistan that required banking products such as agriculture, consumer banking, small and medium sized enterprises, and micro credit. But now paradoxically, these are the areas where we are now investing virtually all their time and energy because they offer a wide scope for product development and a substantial and growing demand for banking services. So, the very substantial improvement in the macro economic situation has enabled. . . .
>
> (Regional Manager 2)

This paragraph in the transcript was coded on two nodes, since it intercepted two ideas; the trend and attitude of the management of banks in the past regarding the banking business, as well as the change and shift in the nature of business due to the improvements in the macro-economic situation faced by the bank. As the coding process progressed, new ideas were discovered and new nodes were created for each of them. Nodes were chosen to reflect the data and concepts or ideas reflected in the analytical framework of the research.

The nodes were revisited and checked for the length of their names and every node name which was three words or more was compressed into one to two words. For example, there was a node called "centralized or a few levels of decision making and people were not empowered". The name of the node was outside the parameter of rule 2 of the coding rules. Thus the node was renamed as "bureaucracy". The next step involved visiting each node and evaluating its importance to the research question/context of the research. The nodes that were found to be not relevant were removed from the coding scheme.

Stage three consisted of going through steps 6–8 which involved checking each node and seeing if any were similar in meaning to one another. For example, nodes called "trigger", "driver", "motivator", and "stimulator" were similar in meaning to one another. Thus, the text coded was combined under one node called "influencing factor". During this process, it was also noted that some nodes were negligible and not important to the research and hence were removed. Once the node meanings were unique, the next step was to group the nodes based on their similarity. This process commenced by combining nodes based on their allegiance to influencing factors of change or resistance/response. For example, the nodes "failed implementation attempt" and "partial implementation of system" seemed more inclined towards "resistance" than towards "influencing factor" and thus were included in the "resistance" group. In the final step, the nodes of the group were clustered together into sub-groups. This was done on the basis of a common meaning being shared by each of the nodes. For example, nodes relating to "design", "implementation", and "use" of PMS were grouped together under the sub-group "change in design, implementation and use". Similarly, other sub-groups were formed under each of the three groups.

At the end of the entire process, twelve nodes were used in each group that directly encapsulated the themes of the analytical framework of the research which mainly included "influencing factor", "pressure to change", "response to change", "employees'" resistance", "frustration", "confusion", "response", "delay", "management commitment", "management support", "dissatisfaction", and "miscellaneous" (used for all other units expressing influencing factors or response or reaction to change). These nodes were essential in many ways. They served as a reminder of the initial thoughts in the analytical framework of the research, as a way to maintain consistency in coding, and to build trustworthiness of the data. Further, these nodes served as a way to create deeper categories of themes (i.e., factors influencing change and responses to such influencing factors) which allowed drawing inferences and making connections among the nodes.

4.7 Validity and reliability of the research

A research study needs to demonstrate that the research is credible and trust-worthy (Patton, 2001; Guba and Lincoln, 1994). There are two main ways of judging the credibility of research, i.e., validity and reliability (McKinnon, 1988).

4.7.1 Validity

Yin (2001) describes validity as the degree to which the results of a research can be generalised to a population other than those studied. According to McKinnon (1988), validity is a factor which any qualitative researcher should be concerned about while designing a research, analysing results, and judging the quality of the research. She further suggests that one way to improve the validity of research is to use triangulation, i.e., obtaining multiple sources of evidence and establishing a chain of evidence during data collection. In this case, the multiple data sources included the use of internal and external documents, questionnaires, and semi-structured interviews. Data triangulation was used as a technique for gathering information in order to obtain different perspectives on the phenomenon investigated. This process enhanced the validity of the findings. Further, to establish a chain of evidence during the data collection period of the research, the researcher also visited the regulators of Pakistan's banking sector (the Regulators) to capture its managers' views, independent of the participants of the research, on the changes experienced within Pakistan's banking context.

Further, during the entire research process, the data collection instruments (questionnaire and interview guide), and the conclusions and findings were reviewed and discussed with a number of senior academics. This enhanced the chances of conducting the research in accordance with the existing research praxis. An attempt was made to increase the validity of the findings in the present research by specifying the context of the empirical investigation. Since a single case has been investigated, the researcher was able to provide the reader with an in-depth description of the case in this book.

Additionally, since interviews involved retrospective information about ten years prior to the interviews, the interviewees' comments were critically analysed and corroborated with data obtained from other sources including internal and external documents, in order to validate their responses.

4.7.2 Reliability

Kirk and Miller (1986, p. 20) state that reliability is about "the degree to which the finding is independent of accidental circumstances of the research". Yin (2003) suggests that it may be valuable to compare reliability with precision. In order to improve reliability, Yin (2003) recommends that a case research protocol and a case research database are constructed. A case research database can be constructed with the aid of a software program, ordinary folders with indexes, or a combination of both. However, there could be threats to the reliability of the research in cases where the main data is classified as confidential due to organisational interest. This is because those outside the case organisation may have difficulties in getting access to some of the documents. In order to address this problem, the research used documents that are not classified. Besides using internal documents, the documents used in the research are publicly available (e.g., State Bank of Pakistan's annual reports, IMF and World Bank's annual reports, Economic Survey of Pakistan, and press releases). No highly sensitive (classified) information is relied on in this case research.

Further, the researcher was given access to interview senior executives of the bank and a meeting was also held with the President of the bank to gain insights into his views on the phenomenon studied. Although the meeting with the bank President was not structured according to the interview guide, it provided his views concerning the changes introduced in the bank. Further, the researcher made every effort to put aside personal values during the investigation and to focus on the interviewees' perceptions of the changes in the PMS.

4.8 Summary

This chapter justified the selection of the qualitative research approach for this research. It also noted the importance of selecting a suitable case organisation and outlined the guidelines used in selecting the case organisation and participants in this research. Furthermore, the chapter clearly demonstrated the importance of using multiple data sources. It describes the data used in the research and also the method used to analyse the data. Finally, the chapter outlined the measures taken to address the threats to the validity and reliability of the research underpinning this book.

Notes

1 Details of the specific financial sector reforms and their implication for banks in Pakistan are provided in Chapter 5.
2 The Management Committee comprised the heads of all Business Groups and functions under the chairmanship of the bank President. Only the President of the bank represents the Management Committee in the bank's Board of Directors. All strategic issues are discussed and approved by the Management Committee prior to the approval from the Board of Directors.
3 Twelve interviews provided the researcher sufficient information to rely on when complemented by the empirical data gathered from other internal and external sources. According to Fossey et al. (2002) there is no minimum or maximum limit of interviews under qualitative research. Interviews with the participants of the research should continue until a saturation point is reached. A saturation point in qualitative research is where facts and information start emerging time and again, and the researcher does not get any new information from the subsequent interviews.
4 Participants were chosen from the Operations, Risk Management, Commercial and Retail Banking, Finance, Audit and Inspection, Organisational Development and Training, Human Resources, Credit and Special Assets Management areas. We have not identified the functional areas of individual respondents in Table 4.1 in order to protect the identity of participants.

5 The external environment of FUB

5.1 Introduction

The purpose of this chapter is to describe the nature of the external environment of FUB and the changes to that environment over the period from 1997 to 2017. Additionally, in order to capture a better understanding of the changes that took place during the period 1997–2017 and the factors that led to those changes, the period from 1995 to 1997 was also examined. The analytical framework of the research, presented in Chapter 3 (see Figure 3.1), will be used to describe and analyse the changes in the bank's external environment. Specifically, the discussion will focus on the three categories of the bank's external environment (political and economic, technological, and socio-cultural) included in the framework. Various documents were reviewed in order to explore the external environment of FUB for the period 1997–2017. The documents reviewed included: (i) annual reports of the State Bank of Pakistan; (ii) speeches of the governors of the central bank; (iii) annual reports of the IMF and World Bank; (iv) the Economic Surveys of Pakistan; and (v) articles published in newspapers and journals concerning Pakistan's banking sector. Additionally, participants' responses to the interview questions were also used to explore and examine changes in FUB's external environment.

The chapter is structured as follows. Section 5.2 presents the background information relating to the banking sector in Pakistan. Section 5.3 then describes the external environment of FUB with three subsections used to describe its economic and political environment, its technological environment, and its socio-cultural environment. Conclusions based on the discussion in this chapter are provided in Section 5.4.

5.2 The banking sector in Pakistan

The banking sector of Pakistan has played an important role in the economic development of the country.[1] Prior to Pakistan's independence in 1947, there were forty-four small-sized domestic banks, mostly family owned, with 487 branches spread all over the territory which now constitutes Pakistan (Ahmed and Amjad, 1984). Shortly after Pakistan's independence, the number of banks and their branches declined to only two domestic banks with 147 branches, as most of the banks shifted their operations to India. In addition, there were nineteen foreign banks, each of which conducted small branch offices. These foreign banks were mainly engaged in financing the export of crops.

There were no formal banking regulations in Pakistan until the end of 1947 to support and govern banks. In the absence of banking regulations, for a few months after Pakistan's independence, the Reserve Bank of India continued regulating and supervising banks in Pakistan under the Companies Act, 1913. However, by the end of 1947, in an attempt to encourage the development of the banking sector in Pakistan, the Government promulgated the Banking Companies Ordinance (1947) with its own banking regulations. In 1948, the State Bank of Pakistan was established as the country's central bank and given responsibility to formulate and implement policies to regulate the banking sector. Following the promulgation of the Banking Companies Ordinance (1947), many new banks were established and the number of branches increased significantly. Further, the Government also established specialised banks and financial institutions with the intention of developing the agricultural and industrial sectors. As a consequence, the number of bank branches increased from 147 in 1948 to 3,418 in 1971 (State Bank of Pakistan, 1999; Khan, 2005). By the end of 1973, there were fourteen banks with 3,423 branches in Pakistan with a further seventy-four branches in foreign countries (Ahmed and Amjad, 1984).

While the increase in the number of banks played a role in Pakistan's economic growth, these banks were severely criticised by the politicians, media, and general public for having concentrated their financing on a few large-scale industries, and for failing to provide resources to the vast agricultural sector (Meenai, 2001). As a consequence, in January 1974, all banks operating in Pakistan were nationalised with the promulgation of the Banks Nationalisation Act 1974 (Ahmed and Amjad, 1984). This was a turning point in the history of banking in Pakistan.

The main objective for the nationalisation of banks in Pakistan was to extend banking facilities on a large scale, in particular, to rural and semi-urban areas (Khan, 2005). After the nationalisation in 1974, all fourteen banks were merged into five (state-owned) banks, thereby creating their complete dominance of the banking business in Pakistan. Under statutory obligations, state-owned banks were required to open new branches to provide banking facilities in remote rural and semi-urban areas which were considered by banks as commercially unfeasible for banking. Nationalisation assured the Government complete control over the banking sector for about two decades from 1975 to 1995 (State Bank of Pakistan, 2000). To coordinate the operations of state-owned banks, the Pakistan Banking Council was set up under Section 9 of the Banks Nationalisation Act (1974).[2]

The Annual Report of the State Bank of Pakistan (2000) indicates that while the nationalisation of banks generated some socio-economic advantages, with banks forced to expand their branch network to remote and underdeveloped areas, their profitability was compromised as it opened the door for unsolicited political interference in banks' decision making. The establishment of the Pakistan Banking Council curtailed the supervisory powers of the State Bank of Pakistan.

The dual supervisory role weakened the independent control of the State Bank of Pakistan over formulating and implementing monetary policies (Meenai, 2001; Khan, 2005). The inadequate and permissive supervision by the Pakistan Banking Council of the state-owned banks resulted in the provision of subsidised loans often on the basis of political considerations, and without adequate guarantees and collateral (Khan, 2005). In addition, successive governments also used banks as job-providing agencies to achieve their political goals. Consequently, most of the state-owned banks were over-staffed with a large number of loss-making branches. Consequently, there was no competitive spirit amongst banks, with more banks developing a culture vested in bureaucratic management, which gradually eroded their image in the eyes of the general public (Khan, 2005; Meenai, 2001). The next section describes the external environment of the case organisation, namely, FUB, and the changes in that environment over the period from 1995 to 2017.

5.3 The external environment of FUB

The literature concerning Pakistan suggests that during the period from 1997 to 2003, there were significant changes in the external environment of FUB. These changes mainly included liberalisation of the banking sector and consequential increases in competition, the adoption of new banking technologies, changes in regulatory frameworks, and turbulent economic and political conditions. This section discusses these factors under three categories, namely, the political and economic environment, the technological environment, and the socio-cultural environment of FUB.

5.3.1 The political and economic environment

The political and economic environment of Pakistan over the last sixty years is a mixture of paradoxes. Politically, the interplay of religious fundamentalism, sectarianism, ethnic cleavages, and regional economic disparities made Pakistan's economy volatile and unstable up to the end of the 1990s (Meenai, 2001; Ziadi, 2005). A review of the Economic Survey of Pakistan (1996, 1997) highlights that Pakistan had seen twenty-three governments in the previous sixty years, including fourteen elected or appointed prime ministers, five interim governments, and thirty-three years of military rule under four different leaders. Excluding the military and interim governments, the average life span of a politically elected government was less than two years. In particular, in the decade prior to 1997, eight different governments ruled Pakistan, four interim-appointed, four elected, thereby heightening the political instability. This instability created an environment of severe economic uncertainty as most of the successive governments reversed key decisions taken by preceding governments on political grounds. Khan (2005) suggests that this persistent political instability led to the economic recession in the late 1990s.

The political instability experienced in Pakistan during the 1990s was associated with deterioration in the economy with the Economic Survey of Pakistan (1996, 1997, 2010) revealing the economic growth declined from six per cent in 1990 to four per cent in 1997, the lowest level in the history of Pakistan since its independence in 1947. The debt burden also increased substantially (from $20 billion in 1990 to $43 billion in 1997), macro-economic imbalances widened, and, worst of all, the incidence of poverty almost doubled. The ratio of debt servicing rose from twenty-three per cent to above forty per cent in 1997 due to the decline in the value of the Pakistani currency. The budget deficit also jumped from three per cent of gross domestic product in 1990 to four per cent in 1997. According to Meenai (2001), by the end of 1997, this external debt burden had become unsustainable.

Iimi (2004) and Khan (2005) note that the persistent decline and uncertainty in Pakistan's economy created a number of structural weaknesses: heavy regulation of the economy with government ownership, industrial licencing, and price controls; a protective trade regime that discouraged competitiveness and export growth; a weak public resource position with an inelastic revenue base, and high current spending with inadequate development expenditure, resulting in excessive budget deficits; high financial repression with public ownership and credit control; and a high and growing burden of (domestic and external) debt, resulting from heavy reliance on borrowing to finance the growth in the mid-1990s.

Pakistan, therefore, had no choice but to enter into a stand-by arrangement with the IMF in the mid-1990s for economic reforms to help the country achieve positive economic growth (State Bank of Pakistan, 2000). The main thrust of these economic reforms was to allow greater freedom to the private sector to own, produce, distribute, and trade goods and services, while gradually withdrawing the public sector from the domestic markets (Meenai, 2001; Khan et al., 2000).

While a wide range of measures was taken to reform the economy, according to the Annual Report of the State Bank of Pakistan (2000), the main economic reforms included:

1 Policy reforms on a broad front, including: (i) trade liberalisation (lower non-trade barriers and an active exchange rate policy); (ii) relaxation of the regulatory framework for industries (investment sanctioning); (iii) economic pricing of inputs and outputs in the agriculture, energy, transport, and public sectors to improve efficiency and public sector resources; and (iv) restructuring the banking sector including capital markets.

2 Restoring the resource balance by improving demand management, including: (i) a reduction of (a) the budget deficit to less than five per cent of gross domestic product, (b) the current account deficit to three per cent of gross national product, (c) inflation to six per cent per year, (d) the debt service ratio to twenty-four per cent of export earnings; and (ii) sustaining the gross domestic product growth rate at over five per cent per year.

As a major component of the economic reforms, the government also decided to restructure the banking sector in Pakistan (State Bank of Pakistan, 2000). As indicated earlier, the poor economic condition in the country plunged the banking sector into serious financial crisis by the mid-1990s, and the Government injected $350 million to offset the losses incurred by state-owned banks (State Bank of Pakistan, 2001). A World Bank Financial Sector Update highlighted the significance of this situation in the following comment:

> in late 1996, Pakistan's banking system was on the verge of a crisis. Non-performing loans had reached alarming proportions. Liquidity problems had begun to emerge as disintermediation spread and banking losses mounted. Most cases of loan defaults remained unresolved in an ineffective court system. Political interference vitiated the financial intermediation function of the banking system and borrowers expected not to repay loans they took, specially from the state-owned banks. Overstaffing and over-branching and undue interference by labor unions in bank personnel and operations resulted in large operating losses. Poor disclosure standards abetted corruption by window-dressing the true picture of banks.
>
> (World Bank, 2000)

The situation of Pakistan's banking sector just prior to 1997 is further articulated in the following comments of the Governor of the State Bank of Pakistan:

> Public sector owned banks dominated the system with its peculiar bureaucratic culture . . . the government of Pakistan was underwriting the losses of these banks out of its scarce budgetary resources. Average lending rate was around 15 to 16 per cent, non-performing loans accounted for almost 25 per cent of total loan portfolio and was a threat to the capital base (as capital to total assets ratio was low), return on assets and return on equity were negative. Most of the banking assets were channeled to the public sector, large corporate and big name borrowers. . . . Foreign banks were busy making money on foreign currency deposits . . . the banking system was dysfunctional and instead of making contribution to the real economy it was acting as a drain.
>
> (State Bank of Pakistan, 2005)

The above views suggest that there were four main reasons for the banking crisis: (i) undue intervention by the government in state-owned banks' key management decisions; (ii) non-performing loans with low recovery rates; (iii) the poor regulatory framework; and (iv) the lack of competition in the banking sector.[3] It was also implied that there was a high level of inefficiency and susceptibility to political pressures and corrupt practices within the state-owned banks (Khan et al., 2000; Khan, 2005). Consequently, state-owned banks remained undercapitalised with hefty loan losses in most of them. For instance, the non-performing loans of all state-owned banks in Pakistan increased from $47 million in 1990 to $1.53 billion or about twenty-five per cent of outstanding loans in 1997 (Khan, 2005).[4] Revamping the banking sector through regulatory changes was of extreme importance, as the health of the banking sector in particular, and the economy in general, was in a state of uncertainty (State Bank of Pakistan, 2001).

Against this background, financial sector reforms were initiated with the support of the World Bank and the IMF, to bring about a paradigm shift in banking regulations.[5] The Governor of the State Bank of Pakistan provided the following rationale for the introduction of the financial sector reforms in the 1990s:

> It was felt and agreed between the Government and the State Bank of Pakistan that major deep rooted reforms had to be undertaken [emphasised in 1997]. As a regulator and supervisor as well as adviser to the Government, the SBP (State Bank of Pakistan) carried out diagnostic studies, prioritized the constraints facing the banking sector, designed the reform strategy and action plan, sought the assistance of the Government of Pakistan and international financial institutions, monitored the progress and made policy, regulatory and institutional changes to facilitate the process.
>
> (State Bank of Pakistan, 2005)

Changes in the regulatory environment

As indicated earlier, the 1997 financial sector reforms in Pakistan included significant regulatory changes which were mainly based on the following principles (Iimi, 2004):

i   To provide functional autonomy to banks and create efficient and productive environments for their operational activities;

ii   To liberalise the entry of private and foreign banks into the banking sector in an attempt to improve efficiency and enhance competition within it;

iii To abolish credit ceilings as an instrument of credit control;

iv   To introduce prudential regulations and corporate governance rules including internal controls and standardised reporting systems;

v   To address the fundamental cause of corruption in banks, poor governance, and financial discipline in state-owned banks;

vi   To change the cost structures of state-owned banks through capital maintenance and increase in public funds;

vii To privatise state-owned banks; and

viii To standardise accounting and auditing systems for banks.

The financial sector reforms commenced in early 1997 and lasted until late 2002. Details of the most notable regulatory changes are summarised in Table 5.1. The government enacted a lot of legislation to empower the regulators to liberalise the sector and simultaneously restructure state-owned banks to inculcate a culture of business-like management and accountability. The objective of these reforms was consistent with the trend in many developed countries where public sector organisations have undergone reform processes and become more accountable for their management actions. In particular, most public sector organisations in developed countries as well as developing countries have moved away from a

Table 5.1 Key financial sector reforms

Year of reform	Area of reform	Reform description
1997	Downsizing and restructuring of banks	State-owned banks were asked to prepare action plans for restructuring and downsizing of their organisations in order to reduce the financial intermediation cost.
	New loan recovery law	In order to provide the necessary legal framework to expedite the recovery of stuck-up loans*, two existing recovery laws, i.e., Banking Tribunal Ordinance, 1994 and Banking Companies (Recovery of Loans) Ordinance, 1997 were repealed and replaced with a new comprehensive law – Banking Companies (Recovery of Loans, Advances, Credits and Finances) Act, 1997.
	Removal of caps on minimum lending rates	Caps on minimum lending rates of banks for trade and project-related modes of financing were removed.
	Basel AccordMinimum paid-up capitalBasel core principles	Banks were instructed to apply the system of risk-weighted capital, in line with the Basel Accord. From December 31, 1997, all banks were required to maintain capital and unencumbered general reserves of not less than 8 per cent of their risk-weighted assets. Effective from December 31, 1997, no bank in Pakistan would carry on business unless it had a minimum paid-up capital of PRs 500 million. This minimum paid-up requirement for banks was doubled in December 2000 to PRs 1,000 million with half of the increase, i.e., up to PRs 750 million to be achieved by December 2002. The State Bank of Pakistan complied with fourteen out of twenty-five core principles (largely compliant in eight and materially non-compliant in three of these principles).
2000	Credit ratings for banks International Financial Reporting Standards	Effective from June 2000, all banks were required to have themselves credit rated by a State Bank-approved rating agency. The State Bank of Pakistan issued directives to banks to prepare accounts in conformity with International Financial Reporting Standards. All banks were required to adopt International Financial Reporting Standards 21, 32, 39, and 40.
2002	CAMELS Framework	The CAMELS Framework was adopted to ascertain the performance of banks on the basis of off-site and on-site surveillance.

Source: State Bank of Pakistan (1997, 2000 and 2002)

*The term "Stuck-up advances" was commonly used in 2000 and refers to "non-performing loans".

bureaucratic mentality to adopt a more business-like approach to management (Perera et al., 2003; Wanna et al., 2003).

(I) REGULATORY CHANGES AND THEIR EFFECTS DURING 1997–1999

As described earlier, the reforms were multifaceted with enactment of laws to liberalise the banking sector in order to establish market-based competition. Liberalisation of Pakistan's banking sector was materialised through an amendment to the Banks Nationalisation Act (1974). The amendments to the Act permitted domestic private and foreign investors to establish banking companies. As a result, twenty-three new domestic private and foreign banks were established resulting in an increase in the total number of branches for all banks from 7,397 in 1990 to 8,673 in 1997 (Khan, 2005). The large expansion in the private and foreign banks' branch network created an intense competitive environment in the banking sector. This enhanced competition provided the major impetus for initiating changes in FUB with all of the questionnaire respondents indicating that the increased intensity of competition in the banking sector forced FUB to initiate changes in its systems, including the PMS.

State-owned banks also had to compete with a large number of non-banking financial institutions.[6] These non-banking financial institutions were given special permission by the regulators to raise deposits through the issuance of certificates of deposit and certificates of investment, while they provided short-term working capital financing and long-term project financing facilities to their customers. The total number of these institutions increased from 36 in 1990 to 156 in 1997 (State Bank of Pakistan, 2000). The comparative position of the number of banks in Pakistan and their branches in 1990 and 1997 is summarised in Table 5.2.

The ownership structure of Pakistan's banking sector changed significantly with a shift from the public sector to the private sector, as revealed in the following comment made by the Governor of the State Bank of Pakistan:

> In Pakistan there was a major shift in the ownership and management of the banking sector after financial sector reforms [in 1997] from a predominantly public sector to the private sector. As a result of liberalization and privatization, 80 per cent of the assets of the banking system are at present in the hands of the private sector.
>
> (State Bank of Pakistan, 2005)

Table 5.2 The number of banks in Pakistan

Category of banks	1990	1997
State-owned banks	5	5
Foreign banks	17	24
Private banks	Nil	16
Non-banking financial institutions	36	156
Number of branches of banks	7,397	8,673

Source: State Bank of Pakistan (1990, 1997)

The increasing competition generated and the pressure that it placed on FUB to make certain changes were explicitly noted by every participant of this research. For instance, a regional manager stated:

> subsequent to liberalisation we saw an increase in competition by many folds. This was an extremely difficult time for us. We decided to get equipped with new technologies . . . which provide a competitive edge . . . [to] make our products competitive. We understood that the bank will not be able to generate business as compared to new competitors . . . the main point was to make sure that we increased the quality of our services and launched new products to increase our market share.
>
> (Regional Manager 2)

Another participant, a branch manager stated:

> there used to be just one bank in this area, where my branch is located . . . but now, there are six different banks . . . most of these are private. We had to improve our customer services, maintain better relationships with them . . . [provide a] broad range of services and technologies.
>
> (Branch Manager 1)

Regulators also placed greater emphasis on corporate governance to improve control systems and to instil a professional culture within banks. Through the amendments to the Banking Companies Ordinance (1962), banks were advised to improve internal controls and corporate governance systems in line with the requirements of the regulators (Khan, 2005). In this context, the Regulation on Banks' Internal Control and Corporate Governance was issued by the regulators in 1997 (revised in 1998 and 2001). This regulation amended the criteria used to appoint members of the Board of Directors, Presidents, and senior management (i.e., Executive Vice President and above), with banks incorporated in Pakistan directed to obtain clearance from the regulators prior to their appointment. Additionally, the appointment of bank Presidents had to be made from a panel of professional bankers maintained by the regulators.

In March 1997, state-owned banks were directed by the regulators to prepare restructuring plans to rationalise their operating activities and size in an attempt to minimise administrative costs. In response, three state-owned banks, including FUB, introduced voluntary separation schemes for employees, and developed plans for branch closure. Within a two-year period, these banks were able to reduce their number of employees from 99,954 to 81,079 by the end of 1999. The number of branches was reduced by 718 from 8,673 branches in 1997 to 7,955 branches in 2000.

To control non-performing loans, banks were directed to classify their loans into four categories, namely, sub-standard, doubtful, loss, and other assets especially mentioned (OAEM), on the basis of the assessment of their risk to the banks. The regulators directed banks to set quarterly recovery targets, submit progress reports, and form strategies to improve future recovery processes. At the same time, minimum conditions for borrowers were also established to ensure that defaulters were not provided any further loans. Banks were also required to provide a list of defaulters to the regulators, those having a total borrowing of PRs 1 million (approximately $10,000)[7] and above, together with details of restructured and rescheduled loans. In order to identify defaulters, the regulators required banks to obtain information from the Credit Information Bureau[8] about total outstanding liabilities of any applicant seeking loans of PRs 0.5 million (approximately $5,000) or more. Subsequently, in 1998, the prudential regulation for loan classification was rationalised, by requiring banks to make qualitative evaluation of their credit portfolios for risk assessment on the basis of adequacy of security, cash flows, and the credit worthiness of borrowers.

In September 1997, all banks were instructed to adopt the system of risk-weighted capital, in line with the Basel Accords. Consequently, effective from December 1997, banks were required to maintain capital and unencumbered general reserves of not less than eight per cent of their risk-weighted assets. In addition, banks had to achieve a minimum paid-up capital of PRs 500 million (approximately $5 million) by the end of December 1998. In December 2000, this minimum capital requirement was doubled to PRs 1,000 million (approximately $10 million). Banks failing to comply with this requirement were subject to being converted into a non-scheduled bank.

(II) REGULATORY CHANGES AND THEIR EFFECTS FROM 2000 AND BEYOND

In order to improve accounting and audit practices within banks and to comply with International Financial Reporting Standards (IFRSs) and International Audit Standards, banks were instructed to adopt IFRS numbers 21, 32, 39, and 40.[9] Banks were required to prepare their financial statements in accordance with these standards effective from the year ending December 2001. In addition, as revealed in the following comment, from early 2002 banks were instructed to report their information in line with the requirements of the newly adopted CAMELS Framework (Table 5.3).

> We have introduced a comprehensive regulatory framework for banks. The framework covers all the necessary performance indicators recommended by BIS [Bank of International Settlements]. Their implementation is ensured through on-site examination and off-site surveillance. . . . And our inspectors specifically verify the compliance of policies and regulations of this framework.
>
> (State Bank of Pakistan, 2005)

Subsequently, in October 2002, in line with the requirements of the Basel Accord conditions, the regulators issued guidelines for managing risks and instructed banks to develop an effective risk measurement and grading system (State Bank of Pakistan, 2002). Banks were advised to measure and report seven

Table 5.3 CAMELS Framework

The CAMELS Framework is consistent with international norms and covers risk-monitoring factors for evaluating the performance of banks. The State Bank of Pakistan enforced six groups of indicators reflecting the financial health of banks.

Capital Adequacy
Capital base of banks facilitates depositors in forming their risk perception about the institutions. Also, it is the key parameter for financial managers to maintain adequate levels of capitalisation. The indicator of capital adequacy is capital to risk-weighted assets ratio (CRWA). According to the Bank Supervision Regulation Committee (The Basel Committee) of the Bank for International Settlements, a minimum eight per cent CRWA is required.

Asset Quality
Asset quality determines the robustness of banks against loss of value in their assets. The deteriorating value of assets, being a prime source of banking problems, directly pours into other areas, as losses are eventually written off against capital, which ultimately jeopardises the earning capacity of the institution. The indicators include non-performing loans to advances, loan default to total advances, and recoveries to loan default ratios.

Management Soundness
Management of a bank is evaluated in terms of capital adequacy, asset quality, earnings and profitability, liquidity and risk sensitivity ratings. In addition, performance evaluation includes compliance with set norms, ability to plan and react to changing circumstances, technical competence, leadership and administrative ability.

Earnings and Profitability
Earnings and profitability, the prime source of increase in capital base, is examined with regards to interest rate policies and adequacy of provisioning. The indicator used to gauge earnings is the Return on Assets (ROA), which is net income after taxes to total asset ratio.

Liquidity
An adequate liquidity position refers to a situation where a bank can obtain sufficient funds, either by increasing liabilities or by converting its assets quickly at a reasonable cost. It is assessed in terms of overall assets and liability management, as mismatching gives rise to liquidity risk. Efficient fund management refers to a situation where a spread between rate sensitive assets (RSA) and rate sensitive liabilities (RSL) is maintained. The tool used to evaluate interest rate exposure is the gap between RSA and RSL, while liquidity is gauged by liquid to total assets ratio.

Sensitivity to Market Risk
The diversified nature of a bank's operations makes vulnerable to various kinds of financial risks. Sensitivity analysis reflects institutions' exposure to interest rate risk, foreign exchange volatility, and equity price risks (these risks are summed in market risk). Risk sensitivity is evaluated in terms of management's ability to monitor and control market risk.

Source: State Bank of Pakistan (2002, 2003)

core risks: (i) credit risk; (ii) market risk; (iii) liquidity risk; (iv) operational risk (mainly: internal control and compliance); (v) legal risk; (vi) reputation risk; and (vii) other risks (mainly: money laundering risk). The risk measurement and grading system provided the minimum standard of risk rating the banks were required to adopt in line with the size and complexity of their business activities. Banks were advised to implement their risk measurement and grading system by December 2003 for all exposures irrespective of the amount. Banks were also advised to submit a compliance report by March 2004 to the effect that the risk measurement and grading system had been put in place. Regulators had the power and the responsibility to monitor each bank's compliance with these guidelines through its on-site inspection and off-site surveillance.

Changes in the regulatory requirements in most OECD countries enabled foreign banks to establish subsidiaries in those countries (Helliar et al., 2002). These subsidiaries promoted competition in the market which, in turn, put pressure on banks to change their organisational structure, business strategies, and management control procedures. Consequently, amongst other changes, FUB was forced to change its systems and procedures, including its PMS, in order to effectively cope with these increased market pressures. This was reflected in the following comment by a business group head.

> back in those days [emphasized, in 1997] adopting a more dynamic role to win new business was crucial . . . this was done by developing new markets for our services. We kept a close focus on our business environment . . . especially the instructions and directives issued by the State Bank. . . . We responded to new regulations by forecasting the direction and intensity of these changes . . . we had no option but to change our structure of our bank, I mean head office and field offices . . . the intensity of change in banking industry . . . forced us to revisit our all businesses, processes, procedures, communication channels, and responsibilities at all levels.
>
> (Business Group Head 1)

Innes and Mitchell (1990), Hussain and Hoque (2002), and Tsamenyi et al. (2006), among others, had similar observations, identifying competition and changes in the regulations as a major factor that motivated change. DiMaggio and Powell (1983) identified these pressures, notably ones imposed by the government and the regulators, as a key source of coercive pressure.

In summary, prior to 1997 FUB's external environment was mainly characterised by political instability and uncertain economic conditions. To address these conditions, the government and the regulators initiated financial sector reforms in 1997. These reforms included issuance of stringent corporate governance guidelines, prudential regulations, liberalisation of the banking sector and new audit, accounting, and internal control requirements. Through these reforms, the regulators forced banks to promote good governance, and a culture of performance and accountability. Almost every participant in this research highlighted the influence of these pressures on FUB which eventually triggered changes in their PMS.

5.3.2 *The technological environment*

Prior to 1997, banks in Pakistan mostly used their branches to provide services to their customers. However, the regulatory changes, described in the preceding section, prompted state-owned banks, including FUB, to redefine their core banking strategy to cope with the increased competition. Almost all of the participants of the research revealed that new private and foreign banks were able to leverage on low-cost banking technologies such as ATMs, telephone banking, and internet banking to reduce their operating costs. Further, they were able to provide their customers with multi-service platforms to conduct transactions through e-banking facilities.

Virtually all of the participants shared the view that during the late 1990s, with the emergence of private and foreign banks, customer preferences for contemporary banking products and services placed increasing pressures on state-owned banks to adopt contemporary banking technologies (State Bank of Pakistan, 2000). This was reflected in increasing numbers of customer complaints against the services of state-owned banks as revealed by a branch manager:

> Customers' complaints were escalating. Generally these complaints were relating to delays in the transfer of funds, long waiting times for withdrawals and the deposit of money at branch counters, poor customer relationship and treatment of customers, frequent errors in billing and account balances, slow and sloppy service, and the lack of ATM and internet services and online platforms for customers' convenience.
>
> (Branch Manager 2)

The results of a national survey, undertaken in 1997 by the Pakistan Bankers Association, suggested that state-owned banks desperately needed to improve customer service and adopt contemporary banking technologies to meet customers' expectations. The survey found that there was an increased demand for contemporary banking products and services, such as ATMs and online banking, with customers expecting efficient, innovative, and value-added products and services. The survey results also revealed that there was a growing urgency for banks to competently manage information systems, management control systems (including the performance measurement), and customer databases to ensure service excellence. The change in customers' expectation was also referred to by a regional manager:

> changes in the Pakistani economy affected the speed of adjustment in Pakistani banks in terms of the demands of customers for good quality services and the move to technology.
>
> (Regional Manager 1)

Pakistan's banking sector responded to the changes in customers' expectations, with the Annual Reports of the State Bank of Pakistan (1996 and 1998) clearly indicating a significant change in the technological environment of Pakistan's banking sector towards the latter half of the 1990s. For instance, during the period from 1996 to 1998, the value of electronic transactions increased by three per cent with a growth of sixty-six per cent in the number of these transactions during the same period. The online branch network also expanded from 134 branches in 1996 to 552 online branches in 1998 (728 in 2000). The banks also increased their ATM network, bringing the total to 1,217 by the end of 1998 and 1,581 by the end of 2000. Furthermore, by the end of 1998 the number of credit, debit, and ATM cardholders had increased from 3.6 million to 4.1 million.

While the progress in creating automated or online branches of banks was quite significant, the State Bank of Pakistan set a clear target for the entire banking sector that by the year 2000 a majority of the bank branches would be online or automated. The State Bank of Pakistan also expected that utility bills payment and remittances would be handled through kiosks or internet banking, reducing both the time and cost for banks. While encouraging banks to adopt e-banking technologies, the State Bank of Pakistan in its annual report (1997) stated:

> Banks have to consider e-banking not only as a technological issue but also as a viable business proposition as the number of internet users in the country is growing exponentially. Banks are encouraged to invest in information technology to enhance efficiency, reduce transaction costs and promote e-commerce.
>
> Use e-banking as an enabler to meet the specific customer needs in service delivery, reduce transaction costs and provide convenience to customers.
>
> (State Bank of Pakistan, 1997)

In summary, the technological environment of Pakistan's banking sector had changed significantly. The new private and foreign banks applied banking technologies such as ATMs, telephone banking, and internet banking to reduce their operating costs and provide their customers with technology-driven platforms to conduct transactions. Further, customer preferences for contemporary banking products and services had also changed which placed pressures on state-owned banks, including FUB, to adopt new banking technologies and competently manage information systems, management control systems, and customer databases.

5.3.3 *The socio-cultural environment*

Since the mid-1990s, there has been a gradual change in Pakistan's socio-cultural environment, with people becoming increasingly conscious of the performance of state-owned banks. The literature concerning Pakistan's banking sector shows that, prior to 1997, the overall banking and financial services penetration rate in Pakistan was generally quite low with Pakistan reporting the lowest number of people per bank branch in the South Asian region. By the end of 1997, only thirty-seven per cent of adults had a bank account and the total numbers of borrowers were 5.5 million, constituting only three per cent of the total population.

There were only 171 deposit accounts and 30 loan accounts per 1,000 persons (State Bank of Pakistan, 2001). This was mainly due to limited awareness and dissemination of banking products and services (Khan, 2005).

Moreover, as described earlier, most of the banks were facing very poor performance due to their excessive loans in comparison to total deposits, having a loan-deposit ratio more than sixty per cent, with continuous escalation in non-performing loans (almost twenty-five per cent of the outstanding loans in 1997) posing a significant threat to the stability of the banking system in Pakistan (Khan, 2005; State Bank of Pakistan, 2000). This inferior performance of banks prior to 1997 also attracted substantial media and general public criticism. Hence, according to Meenai (2001), most of the banks were forced to improve their performance, include internal controls to minimise their exposure to non-performing loans, adopt contemporary banking technologies, increase range of products and services, and improve customer service (Meenai, 2001).

A number of participants of the research also revealed that prior to 1997 the bank's products and services were not tailored to the expectations of many customers with a large segment of society requiring banks to introduce banking products that complied with Shariah (Islamic principles). For instance, a business group head stated:

> due to religious sentiments . . . many people were looking for products which were in harmony with their religious beliefs. . . . Providing Islamic products was an important area to serve genuine needs of many of our customers.
>
> (Business Group Head 5)

Additionally, according to Khan (2005), by the end of the 1990s, bank customers and business and trade associations increasingly questioned the high interest rates charged on lending, and consequently demanded single digit interest rates. In response to the regulator's intervention, banks reduced their interest rate spread to around five per cent from six per cent by the end of 1999 (State Bank of Pakistan, 2003). The decreased interest rate spread was an impetus for the bank to prepare strategies to diversify their product and services portfolio. Explaining the changing expectations of the customers, pressures from trade associations and professional banking bodies, a branch manager stated:

> I think the banking industry in Pakistan was substantially more competitive and innovative by the end of 1997 than it was in 1980s. There are a number of reasons for this which mainly includes deregulation and privatization of the sector. Now we have to compete with a large number of private commercial banks having highly trained and overseas qualified staff. Their branches are located at ideal business places and have highly attractive appearance and layout. They are equipped with latest technology. . . . Their philosophy for marketing deposits schemes is different from us. . . . They make efforts to reach the customers whereas we wait for a customer to come and give us business.

    . . . customer, trade bodies and professional associations are very knowl-
edgeable now . . . they do not compromise on quality of service . . . they shift
their business if they are not satisfied because they have much more options.

                                                 (Branch Manager 2)

In summary, since the mid-1990s, there was a gradual change in Pakistan's
socio-cultural environment with people becoming increasingly aware of banking services in general and the performance of the state-owned banks. The poor
performance of the state-owned banks, in particular increased non-performing
loans, was severely criticised by the media and the general public. Consequently,
most of the banks had become aware of improving their performance, including
internal controls to minimise their exposure to non-performing loans.

5.4 Summary

This chapter outlines the nature of FUB's external environment and the events
which took place in the environment after the implementation of the financial
sector reforms in 1997. The aim of this chapter was to provide the context of
FUB within which the PMS changes took place. As described in the chapter, prior
to the initiation of the financial sector reforms, the banking sector in Pakistan was
mainly dominated by five state-owned banks which were nationalised in 1974.
After nationalisation, these banks operated under a regime of direct government
control with frequent interventions from the government in the banks' key business decisions. These interventions coupled with the weaknesses in the regulatory
system and the lack of governance in state-owned banks, including FUB, eroded
the quality of their assets with widespread loan defaults. Operational inefficiencies due to over-staffing and over-branching also added to the administrative
costs of state-owned banks. Revamping the structure of the banking sector was
of extreme importance, as the banking sector was in a state of uncertainty, which
coincided with the prolonged economic and political instability in the 1990s.
Against this background, in 1997 the financial sector reforms, an external stimu-
lus, were initiated to address the dismal performance of state-owned banks.

    Emanating from the financial sector reforms, several new regulations were
introduced to liberalise the banking sector and to improve management capacity
and accountability mechanisms within the state-owned banks. With the new regulations, the regulators introduced, *inter alia*, prudential regulations, corporate
governance rules, IFRSs, and mandatory credit ratings for banks. These changes
dramatically reshaped the landscape of Pakistan's banking sector in 1997 from
state-owned to private sector and market-based competition.

    With the emergence of private and foreign banks, the technological environ-
ment of FUB also changed significantly. The new private and foreign banks had
applied banking technologies to reduce their operating costs and had provided
their customers with multi-service platforms to conduct transactions through
e-banking facilities. Further, since the mid-1990s, there was a gradual change
in Pakistan's socio-cultural environment with people becoming increasingly

conscious of banking services and the performance of the state-owned banks. Customer preferences for banking products and services had also changed which placed pressures on state-owned banks, including FUB, to adopt contemporary banking technologies and competently manage information systems, management control systems (including the performance measurement), and customer databases.

With the changes in the external environment, in particular regulatory changes and ensuing increased competition from private and foreign banks, FUB was finding it difficult to maintain its market share in terms of assets, deposits, advances, and investments, and thereby created the need for the complete restructuring of FUB's systems and procedures, including the PMS starting in 1997. The next chapter provides a detailed description of the changes in FUB's PMS *vis-à-vis* the pressures generated due to the changes in the external environment described in this chapter.

Notes

1 Pakistan gained independence from British Rule on August 14, 1947. Pakistan is a country located in South Asia that covers an area of 803,940 square kilometers, almost the size of New South Wales, Australia, and a population of 184.753 million. In the south, it borders the Arabian Sea, with a coastline of 1,046 kilometers and stretches north to the Hindukush and Karakoram mountain ranges, with peaks as high as the Nanga Parbat (8,126 meters) and the K2 (8,611 meters). Pakistan is wedged between India, with whom it shares a border of 2,192 kilometers to the east, and Afghanistan and Iran, with whom it has 2,430 kilometers and 909 kilometers, respectively, of common border. It also shares a 523 kilometers border with China in the north.

The socio-cultural environment of Pakistan has its origin in the mixture of many cultures and is reflected in the diversity of different ethnic groups in matters such as customs, languages, and religion. More than twenty local languages are spoken in Pakistan and while Urdu is the national language of the country, English is the medium of education and language of officialdom. Pakistan is the world's sixth most populous country.

Pakistan's principal natural resources are land suitable for farming, water, and natural gas and coal reserves. About twenty-eight per cent of Pakistan's total land area is under cultivation and is watered by one of the largest irrigation systems in the world. Agriculture accounts for about twenty-one per cent of GDP and employs about forty-two per cent of the labour force. The most important crops are cotton, wheat, rice, sugarcane, fruits, and vegetables, which together account for more than seventy-five per cent of the value of total crop output. Pakistan exports rice, fish, fruits, and vegetables and imports vegetable oil, wheat, cotton, pulses, and consumer foods. Cotton textile production and apparel manufacturing are Pakistan's largest industries, accounting for about fifty-two per cent of total exports. Other major industries include food processing, beverages, construction materials, clothing, and paper products. Major imports include petroleum and petroleum products, edible oil, wheat, chemicals, fertiliser, capital goods, industrial raw materials, and consumer products.

2 The Pakistan Banking Council (PBC) was formed under the Banks Nationalisation Act (1974) to perform various functions in line with the objectives of nationalisation, i.e., "to provide for directing banking activities towards national

socio-economic objectives, co-ordinating banking policy and cooperation in various areas of feasible joint activity without eliminating healthy competition in various fields of operation, and ensuring complete security of depositors' funds" (Para. (ii) of preface of Banks Nationalisation Act, 1974).

3 The banking crisis in Pakistan in 1997 coincided with the Asian financial crisis. While the Asian financial crisis affected most of Southeast Asian countries, its impact on Pakistan's banking sector was minimal (Kaufman et al., 1999). None of the participants indicated that the Asian financial crisis had an impact on Pakistan's banking sector and FUB.

4 Pakistan Financial Sector Assessment 1990–2000, State Bank of Pakistan (2000).

5 According to the State Bank of Pakistan Annual Report (2000), the World Bank provided a loan of $200 million in 1997 under the Financial Sector Adjustment Loan. Additionally, a Financial Sector Deepening and Intermediation Project of US$216 million was initiated in 1995 and subsequently another loan of $300 million was secured through the Financial Sector Restructuring and Privatization Project.

6 Development Finance Institutions, Microfinance Banks, Non-banking Finance Companies (including: leasing companies, Investment Banks, Discount Houses, Housing Finance Companies, Venture Capital Companies, Mutual Funds), Modaraba Companies, and Insurance Companies.

7 The amount has been calculated using a AUD1: PRs 86.276 conversion rate as at March 13, 2011.

8 The Credit Information Bureau operates under the control of the State Bank of Pakistan.

9 IFRS 21 (The Effects of Changes in Foreign Exchange Rates), IFRS 32 (Financial Instruments: Presentation), IFRS 39 (Financial Instruments: Recognition and Measurement), and IFRS 40 (Investment Property).

6 Changes in the performance measurement system of FUB

6.1 Introduction

The purpose of this chapter is to analyse the changes in FUB's performance measurement system (PMS) using the analytical framework developed in Chapter 3. The discussion in this chapter revolves around addressing the three research questions of the research: (i) How did the PMS in a bank operating in Pakistan change over the last decade? (ii) What factors influenced the changes? and (iii) How did the bank respond to the factors driving change in the performance measurement system?

As explained in Chapter 5, numerous regulatory changes were introduced in 1997 to reform Pakistan's banking sector. The reforms were introduced against the backdrop of economic recession and political instability in the country. These regulatory changes stimulated major changes in Pakistan's banking sector. The year 1997 was, therefore, seen as a suitable starting point to examine the changes in the PMS of FUB.

The chapter is structured as follows. Section 6.2 provides a description of FUB's background and its PMS prior to 1997. Section 6.3 then examines the factors that applied pressure on FUB to change its PMS. Section 6.4 describes the nature of the changes that were introduced to FUB's PMS in 2000. Section 6.4 also examines FUB's responses to the change. Section 6.5 goes on to identify the pressures that led FUB to adopt a centralised Oracle database in 2003 and describes the further developments in the PMS in the same year. Section 6.6 describes the changes in the PMS in 2003 and beyond. Section 6.7 describes the reaction of employees to the changes in the PMS. Finally, Section 6.8 provides a summary of the chapter.

6.2 FUB prior to 1997

Founded in 1949, FUB was established as the largest state-owned bank in Pakistan with the objective of supporting the government in developing the agricultural and industrial sectors. While FUB operates in a country which adheres to Shariah (Islamic) principles, it is a typical commercial bank which has major businesses in conventional methods of finance and deposits.[1] While the bank was created as a commercial organisation, being owned by the government, its strategy, direction, and business have always kept in line with the government's policy. Thus, its management controls, including its PMS, and working culture were shaped by the government. The bank has always relied on business (i.e., finance and deposits) with the government, as expressed as follows by the President of the bank himself:

> Ninety per cent of our loans were either to the government or public sector. Eighty per cent of our deposits were from government or public sector corporations, so we were a bank totally dependent on the government.
>
> (*The Asian Banker*, 2006)

While FUB grew steadily in terms of its size and resources during the period 1949–1973 the bank faced strong competition from other private and foreign banks. These banks were relatively small compared to FUB, yet they incorporated the latest banking technologies in their operations and had staff with strong banking knowledge and skills. These banks were operating in Pakistan long before the independence of the country in 1947.

However, the nationalisation of banks in 1974 completely wiped out the private part of the banking sector in Pakistan. With the promulgation of the Banks (Amalgamation) Scheme in April 1974, all banks in Pakistan were merged into five state-owned banks. This arrangement eliminated the spirit of competition from the banking sector (Haque and Kardar, 1995). FUB was one of these five banks and enjoyed the benefits of a comfortable business environment under the control of the government.

FUB developed a basic banking culture that focused on deposit-dominated business, and engaged in monetary inter-mediation and traditional "plain vanilla" banking products. Besides this, being a state-owned bank, it rendered public services (often non-revenue based) such as the collection of utility bills, and pension payments to retired government employees and army personnel. With its deposit-dominated business, the bank maintained a banking strategy oriented towards "deposit-growth", and developed a significant deposit collection capability. This was reflected in FUB's heavily deposit-dominated portfolio (seventy-three per cent) and interest/mark-up dominated cost composition (sixty-seven per cent) by the end of 1996 (FUB, 1996, 1997).

In line with its deposit growth banking strategy, FUB's branch network expanded drastically from 17 in 1950 to 1,106 in 1974. The bank continued expanding at the same growth rate after the nationalisation of the banking sector in 1974 with its branches increasing to 1,555 by the end of 1996. Such a persistent growth in branch networks was not unique to FUB, with other state-owned banks in Pakistan's banking sector having between 1,000 and 1,200 branches spread across the country. FUB also established overseas branches and maintained a presence in all major financial centres of the world (i.e., North America, Europe, Central Asia, and the Middle East), although over ninety-six per cent of its total business was conducted within Pakistan (FUB, 1996, 1997).

Prior to 1997, FUB had a branch in almost every city in the country. Some of these branches were established in rural areas which had a very low business potential and viability. Considering the state-controlled nature of the bank, FUB's geographically dispersed branch network appears to have been a response to the need to gain social legitimacy as it was expected that they would provide investment and employment opportunities in remote rural areas. The branch network growth also seems to have been mimetically spurred as such growth was a professional norm for all banks at that time. Comments made by several participants in the research also revealed that most of these branches were established due to pressure from politicians to provide employment opportunities in their electorates so that they could win favour from the general public. For instance, a branch manager made the following comment:

> in those days [Pak]bank was mainly a deposit collecting organisation, . . . opening branches all over Pakistan, not because of business purpose, but because of pressures from the government and certain board members having political links.
>
> (Branch Manager 2)

Another participant stated:

> We had a presence all over the country, particularly in the rural area. Most of these branches were opened without preparing business feasibility. They were opened after receiving instructions and directives from the government . . . the government had their own agenda to win support from the members of the parliament . . . for a government bank like us this type of interference was natural.
>
> (Regional Manager 2)

Given the high labour intensive working conditions in Pakistan, the growth rate in the number of employees in FUB closely corresponded to the rate of growth in its branch network. For instance, starting with 390 employees in 1950, FUB's employees grew from 16,285 to 23,730 between 1974 and 1996. This increase was not unique to FUB, with the number of employees in other state-owned banks also increasing significantly (State Bank of Pakistan, 1996, 1997). Several participants stated that most of the employees were appointed to accommodate requests from the government and the staff unions which were backed by the major political parties in the country. A participant from a regional office (Regional Manager 1) expressed the view that the growth in the number of employees was unplanned, and resulted in overstaffing by personnel with outmoded banking skills. This dilemma was expressed in the following comments:

> Politicians used FUB to provide employment and to subsidise loans to their supporters on political rather than commercial terms, who return the favour in the form of votes and political considerations.
>
> (Business Group Head 5)

The bank was used for the distribution of political favours [employment and loans] because it was relatively easy to disguise political motivations as the bank operates with a large branch network spanning most regions of the country.

(Regional Manager 2)

There were no strict regulatory and audit requirements in the banking sector, although new entrants to the sector were restricted by the Banks Nationalisation Act (1974). According to the participants, the main basis of competition was to mobilise deposits through the expanding branch network with little emphasis on the quality of products and services. Interest rates were controlled by the regulators and the high interest rate spread worked to the benefit of FUB by creating low-cost resources. Consequently, there was no motivation for the bank to innovate and diversify its products and customer services, while the controlled interest rates meant that they had little business risk. In addition, the lack of strict regulatory requirements, in particular financial accountability requirements and the use of independent audit controls, created a business environment that did not require the bank to be overly concerned about the way they carried out their activities. Hence, FUB was not inclined to make any special effort to adopt contemporary banking technologies or management control systems to improve the efficiency of its operations. Consequently, the bank developed an ordinary corporate image as expressed by a business group head:

There were no efforts to bring new business. The bank's top management used to have a government mentality which was reflected in our poor corporate image that we are one of the departments of the government. We never considered ourselves a commercial organisation . . . never focused on providing better customer service.

(Business Group Head 3)

Similarly, the comments of the Governor of the State Bank of Pakistan described the characteristics of state-owned banks in Pakistan prior to 1997:

Public sector owned and managed banks dominated the system with its peculiar bureaucratic culture, indifferent service standards, laid back and lethargic business practices and narrow product range. . . . Professional management, operational efficiency, and strategic direction were by and large missing.

(State Bank of Pakistan, 2005)

The above views portray the corporate image of FUB as an average customer service provider with no strategic business direction. This was primarily due to the presence of a comfortable business environment with no significant competition in the industry and could be attributed to the fact that FUB was primarily dealing with guaranteed business from government and semi-government organisations. Moreover, under the provisions of the Banks Nationalisation Act (1974), the safety of all deposits with FUB was guaranteed by the government.

Similarly to other state-owned banks, FUB's Board of Directors was nominated by the government with the members having civil service and political connections. As a result, according to a branch manager, they were not interested in changing the existing image of the bank or in developing an effective control system (including a PMS) and accountability function within the bank. Formally, the President and the Board of the bank were accountable to the Minister of Finance, and FUB was controlled by way of directives issued by the Ministry of Finance. This situation enabled the government to intervene, often unwarrantedly, in FUB's decision-making processes by enforcing laws, regulations, and rules. In particular, the government in the early to mid-1990s intervened to articulate a formal policy to control credit and employment decisions (Khan, 2005). Such interventions constitute examples of coercive pressure, with the government imposing its power to formulate and enforce laws, regulations, and rules. Such pressures exerted by the government to monitor and control the bank were aimed at promoting its own politically motivated manifestations (DiMaggio and Powell, 1983).

A review of the State Bank of Pakistan's Annual Reports and the comments made by participants of the research revealed that during the period 1990–1996, FUB increasingly faced unwarranted interventions from the government (mainly through the Pakistan Banking Council[2] and National Credit Consultative Council)[3] and labour unions (representing different political parties) in relation to credit and human resource decisions. While such interventions are not unusual in state-owned organisations in developing countries (Uddin and Tsamenyi, 2005; Alam, 1997), they created uncertainty and had a detrimental effect on FUB's operating and financial performance.

A review of the bank's Annual Reports (FUB, 1995, 1996) revealed that by the end of 1996 FUB's financial position had deteriorated significantly. In particular, FUB's market share and profitability eroded alarmingly with the bank's profit falling to $35.71 million in 1995 and declining to its historic lowest level by the end of 1996, a loss of $14.61 million. Its market share declined from twenty-five per cent in 1990 to twenty per cent by the end of 1996. In addition, the assets and deposits of the bank were relegated to third position in comparison with other state-owned banks and the return on assets declined from 0.63 per cent to 0.32 per cent during the same period (FUB, 1995, 1996). In addition, the quality of FUB's loan portfolio deteriorated, resulting in a huge burden of non-performing loans[4] and significant capital impairment.[5] Further, the rapid expansion in the branch network coupled with hurried and ad hoc decisions on staffing, due to the pressures from government and labour unions, resulted in a persistent increase in administrative costs and overstaffing (Business Group Head 4).

The deteriorating financial position posed a threat to FUB's future. The management of FUB realised that the bank's future existence was at stake with a business group head remarking:

> Our operating margin was almost zero. We had a huge problem with the quality of loans and a very high intermediation cost, . . . the morale among staff was low, and all this was reflected in poor customer service, . . . very little balance sheet growth.
>
> (Business Group Head 4)

The following quote from FUB's President was made in reference to FUB's dire situation at the time:

> the greatest apprehension I had when I looked at the balance sheet was that we were so dependent on the government. . . . If we hadn't moved into this commercial and private sector mode, this bank would have sunk.
>
> (*The Asian Banker*, 2006)

Being a main state-owned bank in Pakistan, the poor performance of FUB was heavily criticised by the general public and media, as revealed by a business group head:

> as a public sector bank our performance is always judged by the general public. The bank was openly criticized in the mid-1990s for its depressing performance. . . . There were several editorials published in the national press criticizing our poor performance and service.
>
> (Business Group Head 8)

The interviews with the participants indicated that, besides FUB's exposure to non-performing loans and soaring administrative costs, various other factors also contributed to the bank's poor operating and financial performance. These included imprudent planning, ineffective management control systems, and the lack of strategic direction to mobilise business (deposits and investments), meaning that the bank had failed to identify and control problems as they unfolded. The following comments highlight this predicament.

> planning was ad hoc, with no particular strategy . . . the budgetary control system was never effectively applied. The bank had a performance measurement system for a very long period of time. However, the system was used only to the extent of preparing some management reports at the end of the year and these reports were excluded from the decision making process. . . . I am not aware of any mechanism we used to establish accountability of the senior management . . . no one knew what to use for measuring performance. What I understand is the system was essentially used to provide statistical reports to the State Bank.
>
> (Regional Manager 4)

> Due to the rapid expansion in our business activities and branch network in the 1990s, the performance measurement failed to keep pace with it . . . maybe as a public sector bank senior management was not interested to have a system designed to create accountability of their actions . . . there was no accountability for the senior management because they were government appointees.
>
> (Branch Manager 2)

The above comments provide evidence of the public sector ethos that dominated the culture of FUB. The comments also suggest that the PMS and internal accountability mechanism of the bank played a very limited role in internal controls and that its existence was mostly incidental to the bank's operations.

6.2.1 FUB's performance measurement system prior to 1997

This section of the chapter describes the nature of the PMS and how it was used by FUB prior to 1997.

(i) The nature of the performance measurement system

The PMS used by FUB prior to 1997 was designed to measure the financial performance of the bank's business activities and there was no evidence of the use of non-financial measures during that period. This was revealed in the comments made by many participants and from the review of the internal documents. For instance, a branch manager, in this regard, revealed that:

> In the past we never used non-financial measures. There were a few financial measures used for assessing performance of certain operational activities . . . and this, of course, is what they were designed to do . . . this was typically done on an ad-hoc, piecemeal basis, rather than as an integrated and systematic approach to measure performance.
>
> (Branch Manager 2)

A review of memorandums[6] from the Finance Division to the Management Committee[7] revealed that the bank used only eleven financial measures prior to 1997 (see Table 6.1). These measures were standardised and uniformly applied across all departments at the corporate office, regional office and branch levels irrespective of the nature of their business activities.

To measure performance, the bank prepared a variance report comparing the annual targets and actual results to identify unusual values (variances) that warranted further analysis (see Table 6.2). The variance report was used to gain an understanding of the performance of each business area from a financial viewpoint at the end of each financial year. Using a top-down centralised approach, the Information Resource Management Division within the corporate office was responsible for setting and assigning targets to each business unit after their approval from the bank President. Once approved by the President, the targets were communicated to their respective business units. Performance targets were rigid and usually not reviewed during the year.

(ii) The use of the performance measurement system

A number of participants revealed that the main aim of the measurement system was to measure the efficiency of operations and to track the growth in earnings

Table 6.1 Performance measures – 1997

	Key performance measures
1	Average Deposit
2	Foreign Currency Deposits
3	Non-Fund Bases Income
4	Net Performing Advances
5	Non-Performing Loans
6	Profit/Loss
7	Advances against Exports
8	Advances against Imports
9	Home Remittances
10	Cost of Funds
11	Intermediate Costs

Source: FUB (1996, 1997)

Table 6.2 Performance measurement report

Key performance measures	Actual (Prior year)	Actual (Current year)	Targets (Current year)	Variance 1*	Variance 2**
1 Average Deposit					
2 Foreign Currency Deposits					
3 Non-Fund Bases Income					
4 Net Performing Advances					
5 Non-Performing Loans					
6 Profit/Loss					
7 Advances against Exports					
8 Advances against Imports					
9 Home Remittances					
10 Cost of Funds					
11 Intermediate Costs					

Source: FUB (1996, 1997)

* Variance 1 was calculated to show the current year and prior year comparison (both the amount and percentage)
** Variance 2 was calculated to show the budget to actual comparison (both the amount and percentage)

of each key business unit. The use of financial measures was therefore consistent with the aim of the PMS, as expressed in the following comments.

> We shall dominate Pakistan's financial markets and be the leading bank of Pakistan in terms of assets, deposits and reserves.
>
> (FUB, 1996, p. 1)

> We introduced performance measures mainly to assess operational and financial performance . . . the performance measurement allowed us to view the overall picture of the bank's main revenue earning and deposit related activities. Maintaining or exceeding revenue earnings and deposit targets is critical for [Pak]bank as these two items are very important for our profitability . . . by assessing revenue and deposits, problems and issues can be quickly identified.
>
> (Regional Manager 2)

Several participants also took the view that the general framework for performance measurement was developed to comply with the regulators' requirements to obtain subsidised lines of credit from them. For instance, the amount of net performing advances (net of non-performing loans) and advances against imports and exports had to be reported to the regulators at the end of the financial year to determine the total amount of credit lines from the State Bank of Pakistan. Such compliance is often more likely to occur when there is some degree of dependency, in particular where disclosure is required to secure resources (Oliver, 1991). In the case of FUB, compliance with the regulators' requirements was also crucial to avoid any penalties imposed by them for non-compliance. Furthermore, the imposition of such penalties could have a negative impact on the bank's credibility in the eyes of international financial institutions and local depositors who could have subjected FUB to public and media scrutiny.

Almost all of the research participants suggested that, as a state-owned organisation, and operating in an environment with minimal competition, there was minimal need for effective performance measurement. Furthermore, the performance of business units was not used to establish internal benchmarking or for determining incentives and rewards to individual managers. Instead, a branch manager revealed that seniority played an important role in remuneration and internal staff promotion decisions. For instance, payments as bonuses were made arbitrarily by supervisors, as indicated in the following comment by a branch manager:

> There was no regular incentive system for achieving goals. The incentives were primarily in the shape of cash bonuses which were more dependent on employees' affiliation with the seniors and politically biased staff unions . . . not on the employee's performance.
>
> (Branch Manager 4)

The absence of a measurement culture and performance-based accountability was illustrated in the following comments:

> Measurement of performance has always remained at the top management level . . . there was no use of performance measurement reports. We at lower level were never involved in the measurement process. Employees were not keen to know the outcome of the performance measurement either because

there was no tangible benefit linked with it . . . quite a large number of our loans have defaulted in the past but our management have never made efforts to investigate reasons behind these defaults and the employees responsible.

(Branch Manager 1)

performance measurement was simply another clerical activity . . . we failed to manage and control our poor performance . . . maybe the main reason for this was that we reluctantly used the system in planning . . . controls were missing.

(Regional Manager 2)

Not surprisingly . . . it was fairly difficult to hold managers accountable for the performance of the responsibilities assigned to them . . ., and reward or penalize managers . . . there were many inefficiencies in the performance measurement processes, which, if eliminated, could have yielded significant performance improvements.

(Business Group Head 5)

Similarly, other participants believed that performance measurement was carried out as a matter of routine, and not for any specific purpose. Hence, performance measurement was not a major focus within the context of day-to-day activities and "measuring performance was unnecessary and considered a waste of time" (Branch Manager 4).

There was no evidence to suggest that the President of the bank, who acts as its chief executive officer as well as chairman of the Board, was subject to any performance review and accountability. This was rather typical of an organisation with a predominantly public sector culture and is consistent with the views expressed by Uddin and Tsamenyi (2005).

It was apparent that the PMS was not used by management for planning and control prior to 1997. A participant (Regional Manager 2) stated that the PMS was not of much use because the underlying structure for performance measurement was not established with a proper system to monitor business activities against targets and also because there was no mechanism to regularly review performance and use performance results to improve efficiency. The same participant further observed that the performance reports (i.e., variance reports) were generally not discussed at top management meetings unless there were major negative values. This claim was substantiated by the review of relevant documents which indicated that the variance report was not even prepared in 1996 and 1997, while other reports were merely presented to the Board of Directors at the end of the respective financial year. Moreover, the minutes of the Board meetings provide limited evidence of the extent to which discussion took place pertaining negative variances.

Similarly, regional and branch managers indicated that the variance reports neither added any value nor were used for financial control. They expressed that, despite these reports, FUB continued to incur operating losses and accumulate non-performing loans. As commented by a business group head:

> No attentions were given to variance reports and the results were often buried in files. Producing the variance report was of marginal value to the management because despite taking measures to improve quality of advances, our non-performing loans increased to 22 per cent of total advances in 1997 as against 17 per cent in 1990.
>
> (Business Group Head 5)

Additionally, a business group head, who joined FUB after 1997, adopted the view that when provided, the performance information was rarely accurate and timely. It seems that the variance reports were only fulfilling an internal reporting requirement rather than being used for planning, decision making, and management control. Another participant from a business group revealed that, given top management was generally unaware of many of the complex challenges the bank was facing, the targets were set loosely. This is reflected in the following comments:

> Targets in the reports [variance reports] were developed by someone in the head office. Branch managers always criticized the target setting process . . . they were never heard . . . never given a chance to provide input.
>
> (Business Group Head 1)

Six key conclusions may be drawn from the observations presented in this section:

i   The performance measurement function within the bank was very cursory, focusing on eleven financial measures only;
ii   Performance was measured annually;
iii Performance measurement was unstructured and carried out on an ad hoc basis with no systematic performance review process. Incentives and rewards were not linked to the performance of individuals or business units;
iv   There was no mechanism to measure the performance of corporate office and field offices separately;
v   Information generated from the variance reports was not used for planning and/or decision making; and
vi   The system was not effectively embedded into the bank's culture.

6.3 Pressures to change the PMS: 1997–2000

This section presents the forms of pressures that influenced FUB to change its PMS. In the course of describing these pressures, FUB's strategic responses to these pressures are also discussed. As described in Chapter 5, there were significant changes in FUB's external environment prior to 1997, in particular, characterised by political instability and uncertain economic conditions. These external environmental conditions led to changes in FUB's regulatory environment (i.e., institutional environment) and forced it to make changes in its systems and procedures, including its PMS. The participants' responses and the documentary evidence reveal that these changes, as illustrated in the analytical framework of this research, occurred through coercive, mimetic, and normative pressures.[8] Some of these pressures are found to have greater influence than others, as revealed in the participants' responses and documentary evidence.

6.3.1 Coercive pressure

Coercive pressure is clearly present in the form of regulatory changes in Pakistan's banking sector. Directives from the Board of Directors and the new President of the bank also provided an additional pressure to promote efficiency, performance, and accountability within FUB.

The financial sector reforms initiated in 1997 coerced banks in Pakistan, including FUB, to introduce changes in PMSs. As discussed in Chapter 5, from the mid-1990s, changes in the banks' external environment had placed Pakistan's banking sector in a severe crisis. In response to this crisis, the government initiated the financial sector reforms in 1997. Through these reforms the regulators made a number of regulatory changes to enhance the efficiency and effectiveness of state-owned banks and to improve their control systems. These regulatory changes included the introduction of stringent prudential regulations, guidelines for corporate governance and internal controls, and a framework for effective risk assessment and mitigation (see Table 5.1).

Under the new regulations, the scope of the required performance information in relation to non-performing loans was expanded from that required previously.[9] The aim of this regulation was also to improve the quality of the banks' loan portfolios and to minimise provisioning against these loans or loan write-offs (State Bank of Pakistan, 2000). Specifically, FUB had to change its PMS to classify non-performing loans using four categories of performance measures and send reports to the regulators for examination. A review of the 1997 and 2000 Annual Reports (State Bank of Pakistan, 1997, 2000) indicates that banks in Pakistan were required to measure the quality of loans using four categories of non-performing loans, namely, (i) sub-standard, (ii) doubtful, (iii) loss, and (iv) other assets especially mentioned (OAEM). Prior to 1997, FUB had only been required to calculate bank-wide aggregate non-performing loans without considering the age of the overdue loans. Banks were also directed to set recovery targets against non-performing loans for each of the categories, submit progress reports, and form strategies to improve future recovery processes (State Bank of Pakistan, 1997). The directives from the regulators clearly coerced FUB to introduce new performance measures in an attempt to (i) mitigate non-performing loans and (ii) strengthen accountability towards achieving targets against the recovery of non-performing loans. Eleven of the twelve respondents to the questionnaire indicated that the changes in the "Central Bank's regulatory controls" influenced the changes in their performance measures to a great extent.

To improve corporate governance practices in Pakistan's banks, the new regulations required them to appoint Board Directors and senior executives who met a new "Fit and Proper Test".[10] The regulation on corporate governance expanded the role of the Board of Directors to internal control and risk management, supervision, and internal audit. To comply with this regulation, in 1997, the government changed FUB's Board of Directors by nominating members from the private sector with a banking and financial background. Under the new composition of the Board, with the exception of the President of the bank who also acts as the chairman of the Board, all other members were non-executive. Participants of the research observed that the inclusion of Board members from the private sector was seen to reduce unwarranted influence from government, politicians, and labour unions.

The new Board of Directors first met in 1998 and expressed concern over the poor performance of the branches. The Board directed management to develop clear objectives and policies to strengthen the branches' financial and operating activities and specified that a report on the profitability of all branches would be required for every Board meeting. The aim of this directive was to monitor the profitability of the branches and to identify loss-making branch operations (Regional Manager 2). A business group head and a branch manager, in this context commented:

> Profitability of our business at branches was a major point of worry when the new President took over the Bank. . . . The Board on the [new] President's recommendation introduced profitability reporting to head office . . . these reports became an important part of the Board of Directors' agenda.
>
> We changed some branch managers because they failed to achieve profitability targets assigned to their branches. . . . Some of the branches were either closed permanently or merged with others after the introduction of this report.
>
> (Business Group Head 7)

> reporting branch profitability was a directive from the Board. The Board wanted to monitor profitability and operating cost of the branches which was one of the major problem areas of the bank . . . the Board wanted to close all such [loss making] branches.
>
> (Branch Manager 2)

Additional coercive pressures were attributed to the appointment of a new President in 1998 who was mandated by the government to assess FUB's current position and restructure the bank into a self-contained commercial set-up.[11] According to a participant (Business Group Head 4), the new President was given full autonomy and legislative powers to make decisions without any interference from the government, political parties and staff unions. The same participant also described that, prior to 1997, the President of the bank was understood to be the "government's man" and expected to be a quasi-bureaucrat whose most valuable skills used to be "government relations" and "political skills". Soon after his appointment, the new President took a number of measures, including (i) appointing new business group heads, (ii) commencing a detailed review of FUB's operations by appointing a task force and an external consultant, and (iii) initiating changes in the organisational structure. The results of the questionnaire indicated that the new President and the Board of Directors were instrumental in initiating the changes to the performance measures in FUB.

(i) The appointment of new business group heads

In early 1999, the new President obtained approval from the regulators to replace the heads of four out of the six divisions (i.e., commercial banking, credit and treasury, human resources, and performance measurement and budgeting) with professionals possessing extensive experience in managing foreign banks in Pakistan.[12] Participants of the research claimed that with these changes the new top management intended to consolidate its power by appointing like-minded people to key positions so as to be able to implement strategic changes with minimum resistance and uncertainty during the process of change. In FUB, the possibility of some degree of resistance from existing employees was implied in the comments made by the participants of the research. In particular, the four divisional heads replaced had been working with the bank over a long period prior to 1997, and were perceived as likely to have had difficulty in coping with the potential changes. A participant stated that:

> We were expecting some resistance from employees who were with the bank over a prolonged period before the restructuring. They had a lower level of education and banking qualifications. Most of them were office bearers of the staff union . . . the management admitted that they had difficulties . . . they were under stress and restructuring was unsettling and disruptive for them.
>
> (Business Group Head 3)

(ii) A detailed review of FUB's systems and procedures

Immediately after the appointment of the new group heads, the new President organised a series of meetings with the divisional, departmental, and provincial heads to communicate the bank's intention to initiate organisational restructuring. While providing the rationale for this restructuring, the President expressed the following views:

> there were many levels of decision-making, and people in the field were not empowered. There was very little in the way of training for employees and the culture of merit was in a sense absent because there was much more emphasis on seniority. There was very little information technology and our IT platform was very basic, which is why we could not bring in new products and improve our delivery system.

. . . the decision-making process was laborious and very slow. Decisions would take anywhere from 100 to 120 days to be made. Obviously you cannot sustain a service organization when the decision-making is slow and impeded. So we worked on two fronts. We substantially reduced the decision-making stages from seven down to two.

We empowered people in the field. Previously, 80 per cent of decision-making was made at the head office. When we restructured, we tried to ensure that at least 60 per cent of the decisions were made in the field. Our ultimate objective is that 90 per cent of decisions are made in the field within a three-year period, while the head office becomes a central support centre and much smaller in terms of size and cost.

(FUB, 2004)

The main concern highlighted by the President stemmed from inefficiencies in the organisational structure, business strategy, and decision-making processes. A participant from a regional office (Regional Manager 1) suggested that the President responded to these inefficiencies by adapting both FUB's organisational and field structures, not only to increase efficiency but also to raise accountability awareness in what had previously been a strictly bureaucratic public sector organisation. The President's main aim was to change the way in which employees perceived their work and to ensure they interacted internally and responded to the external environment efficiently and effectively. Another participant (Business Group Head 5) observed that the new President wanted to make employees more accountable and responsible for their actions and performance. He also suggested that the President sought to change the organisational structure to strengthen FUB's profitability and its corporate image, and to create a more market-oriented organisation which could meet post-reform competitive pressures. The importance of adapting organisational systems and procedures to the changing management expectations in order to be effective has been widely recognised in the management accounting literature (Dent, 1990; Simons, 1990; Langfield-Smith, 1997). Such adaptation eventually creates a need for change in other systems, including PMSs (Hussain and Hoque, 2002).

Consistent with Oliver's (1991) arguments, the above comments also imply that with the initiation of organisational restructuring the President attempted to secure legitimacy from its institutional environment as such initiatives were expected from him by the government, the regulators, and the general public. According to Business Group Head 7, being a main state-owned bank in Pakistan, FUB's performance was always being judged by society and had been heavily criticised in the past due to its poor performance. Further, the bank also appears to have used organisational restructuring in an attempt to change the "public sector" image which was largely characterised by operational inefficiency and low quality products and customer services.

According to Oliver (1991), when organisations plan to overcome internal organisational inefficiencies, they tend to carry out a review process to demonstrate that they are addressing the concerns of the institutional environment. In mid-1999, the President initiated a detailed review of the bank's management systems, including its PMS, by forming a task force selected from the Management Committee. The task force had an important role in the restructuring and image building of FUB. Regional Manager 1 noted that such image building was crucial at that point to build the confidence of depositors and borrowers by exhibiting that the bank valued customer relationships and a quality consciousness ethos, and was no longer organised as a government department. An external consultant was also engaged to provide guidance during the review and to search for best banking practices that could be adopted by FUB's management.

(iii) Changes in the organisational structure

In late 1999, following the recommendation of the task force and the external consultant, the President changed the organisational structure of the bank. A review of FUB's Annual Reports (FUB, 2000, 2001) indicates that, prior to 1999, the bank had a five-level, hierarchical structure base and used a multi-layered decision-making framework which focused on core functional areas. While discussing changes in the organisational structure, Business Group Head 4 revealed that the complex hierarchical structure that existed prior to 1999 led to communication and decision-making problems across different divisions, provincial offices, and branches. This problem was also noted by the head of the business group as follows:

> The decision process was laborious and very slow. Decisions would take anywhere from 3–4 months to make.
>
> (Business Group Head 8)

Participants at all levels indicated their understanding that, as the new business strategy required greater autonomy and timely decision making, management had decided to abandon divisions and provincial offices and to introduce a structure where the bank was reorganised into independently functioning autonomous business groups. Figure 6.1 illustrates the new and old organisational structure.

The new organisational structure was flatter with clearly defined management responsibilities and accountability. Under the new organisational structure, the bank used a profit centre approach with field offices (regional offices and branches) reorganised geographically. In addition, a new sub-unit (namely, the Performance Measurement and Budgeting Department) was formed with clearly defined responsibilities to coordinate and support the performance measurement and financial planning function within the bank. While describing changes in the organisational structure, Business Group Head 3 expressed the view that the work patterns in branches were revamped to make them independent and self-contained so as to enable them to make decisions based on their local circumstances. This was critical to ensure a strong coupling between the new strategy and business processes, as observed by Business Group Head 4. The objective, as stated by Business Group Head 6, was to develop branches into

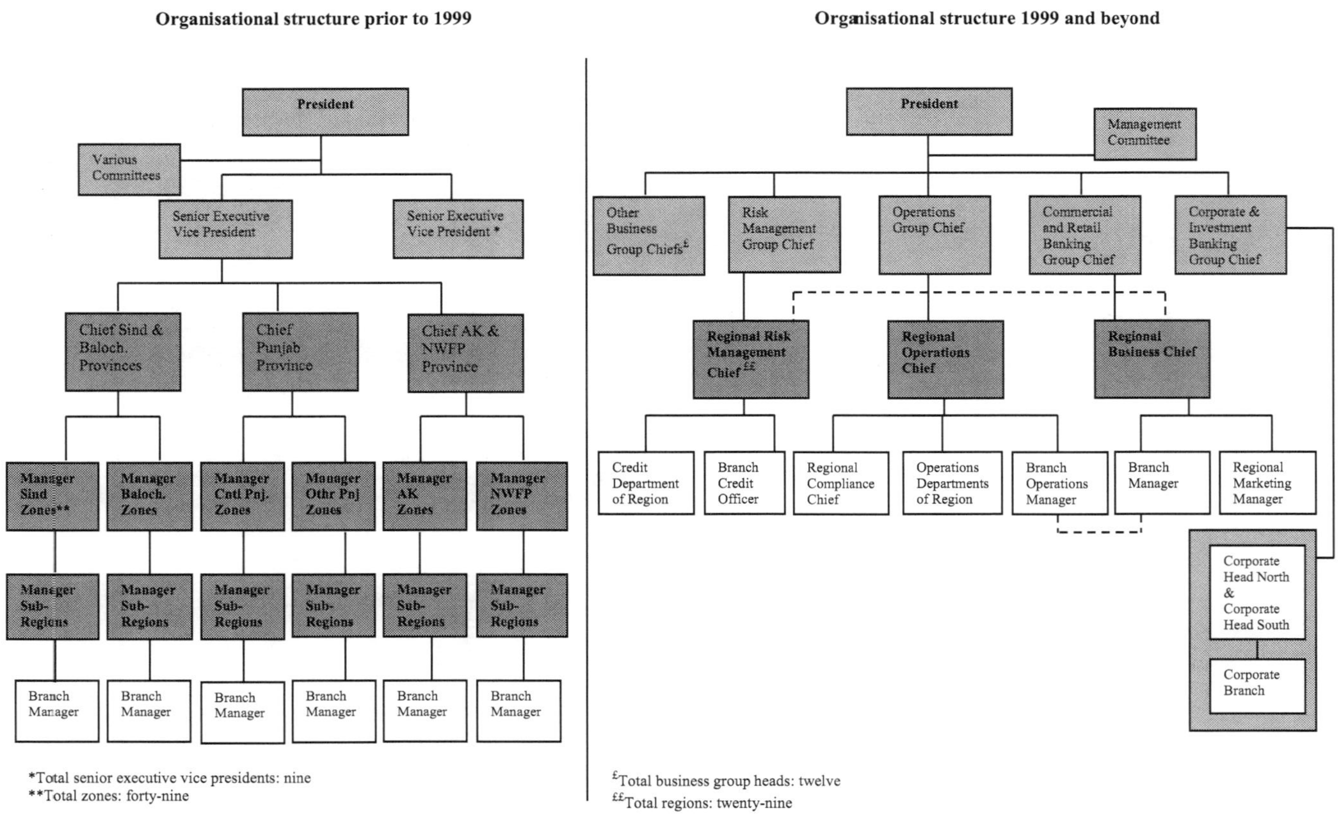

Organisational structure 1999 and beyond

Management Committee

President

Other Business Group Chiefs[£]

Risk Management Group Chief

Operations Group Chief

Commercial and Retail Banking Group Chief

Corporate & Investment Banking Group Chief

Regional Risk Management Chief[££]

Regional Operations Chief

Regional Business Chief

Credit Department of Region

Branch Credit Officer

Regional Compliance Chief

Operations Departments of Region

Branch Operations Manager

Branch Manager

Regional Marketing Manager

Corporate Head North & Corporate Head South

Corporate Branch

[£]Total business group heads: twelve
[££]Total regions: twenty-nine

Organisational structure prior to 1999

President

Various Committees

Senior Executive Vice President

Senior Executive Vice President *

Chief Sind & Baloch. Provinces

Chief Punjab Province

Chief AK & NWFP Province

Manager Sind Zones**

Manager Baloch. Zones

Manager Cntl. Pnj. Zones

Manager Othr Pnj. Zones

Manager AK Zones

Manager NWFP Zones

Manager Sub-Regions

Manager Sub-Regions

Manager Sub-Regions

Manager Sub-Regions

Manager Sub-Regions

Manager Sub-Regions

Branch Manager

Branch Manager

Branch Manager

Branch Manager

Branch Manager

Branch Manager

*Total senior executive vice presidents: nine
**Total zones: forty-nine

Figure 6.1 A comparative position of FUB's organisational structure pre- and post-1999

the "one-window" for a range of services, and the first point of contact for customers. Furthermore, some activities that had evolved without a clear purpose, such as providing a Daily Activity Report for Head Office, were removed. These reports, as revealed by Business Group Head 3, were never used for performance measurement purposes. Substantiating this claim by the business group head, another participant of the research, a branch manager stated:

> Several activities were not clear in terms of its use . . . they were part of the bank [undertaken by the bank] since a very long period and had problems . . . they have no clear purpose and were clear duplication. These duplications were removed because there was no benefit in retaining them. Undertaking them was sheer waste of time.
>
> (Branch Manager 1)

With its new organisational structure, business groups were supported by the field offices (i.e., regional offices and branches) and two layers of management were removed in order to delegate more authority and responsibility down to lower level operational managers. Many participants of the research believed that this empowerment of operational managers, who were given enhanced financial and decision-making responsibilities, warranted rigorous performance measurement and controls. For instance in the survey eleven of the twelve respondents indicated that the change in management style, with more empowerment of managers at the lower level, necessitated the improvements in performance measurement and controls within FUB.

Two participants (Business Group Head 5 and Branch Manager 2) also observed that FUB sought to use performance measures which would reflect operational efficiency, such as "assets utilisation" and "cost of funds mobilised". These performance measures were needed to increase profitability and improve cost control. The participants also believed that the bank wanted to have a performance measurement process that enabled management to continuously monitor performance and control problems before they unfolded. From the participants' perspective, the empowerment of employees at middle and lower management levels created a sense of internal competition amongst regions, branches, and individual branch managers, leading to improved decision making and accountability. This was illustrated by the following comment of a business group head:

> since we had a large number of loss-making branches therefore, to improve their performance we created a sense of autonomy by empowering them to take decisions independently. This was done because we wanted to establish competition amongst them and to develop internal benchmarking.
>
> (Business Group Head 6)

The foregoing comments by the participants indicate that the changes in the organisational structure made the bank a more complex entity. It led to the delegation of authority and responsibilities down to the lower management level, flattened the decision-making hierarchy, redefined employee roles, and created new positions. Several participants recalled:

> the new organisational structure integrated functional boundaries within [Pak]bank which had significant impact on the work patterns, managerial responsibilities, roles, job descriptions, delegation of financial powers and change in market territories . . . for this reason we sought to have improvements in our performance measurement.
>
> (Business Group Head 4)

> this change was indeed very compelling to believe that changing performance measurement is necessary . . . in new structure for field offices [branches], learning about customer satisfaction and quality of our service was critical because the branch managers were accountable for the business targets assigned to them. In the past this was not evaluated because business from the Government was guaranteed and assessing performance under such circumstances was of no use.
>
> (Branch Manager 2)

> After restructuring our responsibilities increased by many folds with more decision making power . . . managers became more independent and accountable for their actions . . . the performance measurement was not able to meet these new requirements . . . the performance measurement process was extremely outdated.
>
> (Regional Head 2)

Most participants in the research indicated that these changes made the PMS obsolete and inadequate. This finding is also substantiated from the responses of participants to the questionnaire which shows that ten out of twelve participants identified delegation of responsibilities together with the diversification in FUB's business activities as an important factor that made the existing PMS redundant. All participants held the view that the changes in the organisational structure required FUB to change its existing performance measurement process and the types of performance measures used to assess the performance of corporate office, regions, and branches. A regional manager (Regional Manager 2) observed that as management delegated financial and operational decision-making power to lower management, they required more elaborate internal controls and performance measurement which could not only focus on the effectiveness and efficiency of operations, and the reliability of reporting, but also compliance with regulations. This finding is consistent with several other management accounting studies (e.g., Yazdifar et al., 2008; Tsamenyi et al., 2006; Waggoner et al., 1999). The existing literature also suggests that changing organisational structure and strategy can provide the necessary pressure to drive changes in management accounting practices in organisations, including their PMSs (Hussain and Hoque, 2002; Marginson and Considine, 2000).

The participants clearly indicated that with the regulatory change and consequential adaptation of the structure and strategy, FUB needed a more comprehensive PMS to improve its operational and financial controls. While reflecting on the need to change, several participants indicated that the new top management wanted to induce a rigorous strategic planning and performance measurement process throughout the bank. For instance, a business group head (Business Group Head 4) indicated that the use of a systematic strategic planning and performance measurement process would enable FUB to capture a more comprehensive view of its business activities and consequently enhance its capacity to adopt the performance measurement function more effectively. Similarly, a business group head (Business Group Head 2) emphasised that the newly appointed President voiced concerns about the existing performance measures. A major point of his concern was that the PMS inadequately considered performance drivers that would assure future business given the rapidly changing external environment of the bank. These comments also imply that, over time, the PMS had become less useful as the objectives of the bank changed along with the activities to be measured relating to the business processes, functions, and their relationships. A business group head (Business Group Head 6) revealed that the performance measures in the bank were set as indicators of activities not of outcomes. For example, a measure like non-performing loans was applied to the aggregate amount of loans in default or not performing at the end of a financial year. It neither measured the effect of the recovery efforts nor the efforts of the relevant staff in recovering the non-performing loans. These views were substantiated by a participant from the regional office as follows:

> We wanted to have measures of performance to go beyond costs and profits . . . we were required to deliver services cost-effectively and according to priorities established in corporate plans . . . this was not possible with existing measures.
>
> (Regional Manager 2)

The dissatisfaction of top management towards existing systems has been identified in the literature as a key factor that influences management accounting change (Innes and Mitchell, 1990). As noted earlier, the dissatisfaction of FUB's top management can be attributed to the increased complexity of the bank's external environment. The change in that environment made top management more conscious of the importance of improving the bank's performance measurement function. In the absence of external environmental changes, i.e., the uncertain economic and political conditions and the ensuing regulatory and competitive pressures, FUB would not have been inclined to change or improve its PMS. Similar views are also presented in other management accounting studies, such as, Yazdifar et al. (2008), Hussain and Hoque (2002), Cobb et al. (1995) and Innes and Mitchell (1990).

Oliver (1991) suggests that coercive pressures, such as the regulatory directives described in this section, limit organisational choices. Under such pressures, organisations choose to comply passively with institutional expectations in order to survive (Oliver, 1991). In accordance with Oliver (1991), FUB might be expected to offer a less active response to the pressures generated by the regulatory changes. Compliance was the most likely response because, in the case of FUB, the benefits for complying were much more favourable for its survival when compared to a non-compliance response. Oliver (1991) suggests that the advantages to compliance are many, for instance, "increased prestige, stability, legitimacy, social support, internal and external commitment, access to resources, attraction of personnel, fit into administrative categories, acceptance in professions, and invulnerability to questioning" (Oliver, 1991, p. 150). In this case, the bank complied with the regulatory requirements to secure legitimacy from the regulators by avoiding any financial penalty for non-compliance.

6.3.2 *Mimetic pressure*

Mimetic pressure was also instrumental in influencing FUB to introduce changes in its PMS. In particular, following the appointment of a new President and new business group heads, the formation of a task force, and the appointment of an external consultant, FUB attempted to adopt best banking practices. The bank also focused on introducing contemporary banking products and adopted innovative banking technologies by modelling other private and foreign banks.

Pressure to adopt best banking practices

A review of the minutes of meetings revealed that in undertaking the review of FUB's management systems the task force and external consultant considered the structure, strategy, and performance measurement practices of other banks. Specifically, representatives from foreign banks and the Central Bank were invited to share their experiences at Management Committee meetings, as revealed in the following comments.

> [Pak]bank considered the practices of the other banks particularly foreign banks. We also had a comprehensive research of the recent structural and management change in the Central Bank.
>
> (Regional Manager 2)

> The bank undertook search for the best practices being used by the foreign banks because their systems are time tested and developed by highly professional and trained bankers.
>
> (Business Group Head 1)

The above comments suggest FUB's eagerness to mimic the structure, strategy, and performance measurement practices of other banks as they were perceived to be more legitimate and/or highly successful (Meyer and Rowan, 1977). Meyer and Rowan (1977) also suggest that under uncertain conditions, as was the case in Pakistan's banking sector in 1997, organisations strive for legitimacy because the systems being used by them are either not suitable or are not adequate for them. Thus, in such situations, organisations seek to adopt systems that are acceptable to their stakeholders. DiMaggio and Powell (1983) suggest that such behaviour by organisations makes them increasingly isomorphic to other banks. FUB's environment was both competitive and rapidly changing, making it vital for them to meet stakeholders' expectations to gain legitimacy.

From the participants' viewpoint, the new organisational structure was identical to those of the private banks operating in Pakistan. Regional Manager 1 observed that such an organisational structure was considered as standard in all private and foreign banks in Pakistan and perceived as better by the new top management to support the new business strategy. In terms of institutional theory, when an organisation realises that most of its competitors adopt industry standards, it tends to adopt similar standards in order to achieve legitimacy from its constituents, both internal (employees and the Board of Directors) and external (depositors, borrowers, government, and the regulators) (DiMaggio and Powell, 1983).

As noted in the preceding section, while changing its organisational structure FUB also de-layered its field structure with the old forty-nine zones replaced by twenty-nine new regions. Similarly to the operations of foreign banks, the regional offices and branches were split into "operations" and "businesses". Several participants of the research, in particular, Business Group Head 6 and Regional Manager 1, stated that the operational structures being used by the foreign banks were, to a large extent, promoted by the new top management, in particular by the President. While further elaborating this point, Business Group Head 6 stated that the new top management perceived the operational structure of the foreign banks as superior and exceptionally comprehensive. Consistent with the argument extended by DiMaggio and Powell (1991), the observance of foreign banks' operational structures resulted from mimetic isomorphism, which encourages organisations within an industry to adopt similar practices to make them more alike. Under the new structure, the distribution of branches to regions changed their authority and responsibility, and their reporting lines. A dual reporting system was introduced. Moving away from one regional chief, which delayed decision making, the management of field offices was further de-layered to three regional chiefs, namely, regional business chiefs, regional operations chiefs, and regional risk management chiefs (see Figure 6.2).[13]

Focus on contemporary banking products and technologies

As explained in Chapter 5, there was rapid growth in the number of private and foreign banks and branches, and while most of the new entrants were smaller than FUB, the effects of their presence were still noticeable. The participants revealed that the new entrants were much more aggressive in marketing their products and services, and were equipped with contemporary banking technologies, such as online banking, credit cards, debit cards, and consumer banking. Regional Manager 1 observed that they instituted new norms in Pakistan's

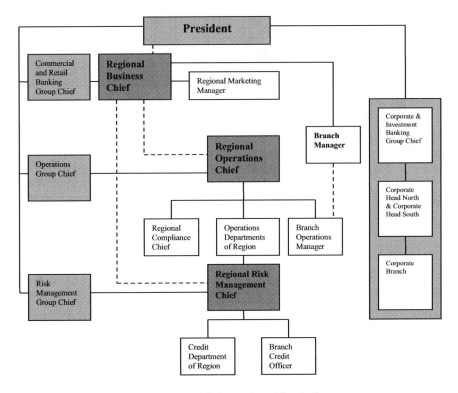

Figure 6.2 Revised field structure of FUB 1999 and beyond
Source: FUB (1999, President's Office Circular No. 19, Head Office, pp. 1–7)

banking business, norms characterised by contemporary banking technologies and efficiency in customer services. DiMaggio and Powell (1983) argue that such technological changes in an organisational field, in this case Pakistan's banking sector, can become a source of mimetic isomorphism, with organisations pressurised to adopt similar technologies. Business Group Head 5 observed that the adoption of such banking technologies to provide quality products and services was expected from FUB by its customers. In this regard a regional manager expressed:

> the private banks had modern banking technology and management techniques which enhanced the quality and sophistication of the financial services offered to the public in Pakistan. All banks wanted to use similar type of technologies. . . . Our customers expected similar banking services from us.
> (Regional Manager 2)

The increased competition associated with the entry of new private and foreign banks affected FUB's profitability and market share. This situation made it difficult for FUB to compete using its existing traditional banking products and technologies. A participant (Business Group Head 8) recalled that the increased competition in the banking sector placed FUB under immense pressure to diversify and innovate in regard to its products and to adopt contemporary banking technologies. For instance, one of the participants from a branch stated:

> The banking sector in Pakistan is now highly innovative with more products such as credit cards, online transfers, EFTs, and internet banking than in the 1980s and early 1990s. This change was mainly due to deregulation, liberalization and resulting increases in competitiveness in the banking sector.
>
> (Branch Manager 1)

Another participant, a business group head from the corporate office, highlighted the importance of adapting to the changed banking environment and repositioning the bank's resources, systems and business profile:

> It was crucial for [Pak]bank to adopt new banking systems to address current business and environmental needs. This was very challenging because the banking sector in Pakistan was rapidly changing . . ., many new players had entered in the sector with much better banking solutions and technologies. Our survival was only in responding to these changes and new challenges by improving the bank's systems, services to customers and relationships with them, the look of the branches and anticipating customers' expectations. Without this response our existence in the market was not easy.
>
> (Business Group Head 1)

The growth in FUB's range of products and services meant that it had greater requirements for market information, data concerning depositors and borrowers, and measuring performance and controls. In particular, measuring performance using eleven financial performance measures for each business unit was becoming unmanageable due to the complexity and requirements of the new information and data. Thus, as observed by Business Group Head 5, the need to change the PMS arose in order to diversify the information provided to measure performance across all business units. Furthermore, Participants also referred to a number of problems with the eleven performance measures used prior to 1997, as reflected in the following comments:

> there was a need for separate measures for the head office and branches. This was quite obvious because the activities of the head office are different from branches . . . the nature of business activities in branches at rural areas was significantly different from the corporate office . . . the branches in rural area are small in size and most of them never operate on commercial lines.
>
> (Branch Manager 2)

> in the past performance targets were set without considering ground realities, skills, and resources available with the bank . . . it was necessary for [FUB] to have a different type of performance measurement process and

control system. The system was not suitable for a commercial organisation like [Pak]bank.

(Business Group Head 6)

the system was not accommodating new regulations and change in other interrelated systems of the [Pak]bank. The system was top management driven, imposed on regions and branches. Most of the branch managers in their daily jobs were not in any way involved in performance measurement function. Traditionally performance measurement was solely the responsibility of the head office.

(Branch Manager 1)

The above comments by the participants clearly indicate that changes to the PMS were crucial for FUB in order for it to compete and survive in a highly competitive environment. According to Business Group Head 4, FUB's management became conscious of the need to change the bank's management systems and business strategy to cope effectively with the market pressures and changed expectations of the external stakeholders, in particular, the regulators and customers. The bank seems to have recognised that failure to respond quickly to such pressures could result in a loss of business from depositors and borrowers, thereby potentially losing social legitimacy. In this regard FUB's President stated:

we were a public service organisation when we were a nationalised bank and prior to the initiation of the financial sector reforms. But this institution would have collapsed if it had not transformed.

(*The New York Times*, 2004)

6.3.3 Normative pressure

Normative pressure is associated with professionalism and was exerted through the education and/or training received by organisational members, which enhanced their ability to develop and promote new rules, systems, and routines within the organisation. In FUB these pressures were mainly generated following the implementation of a comprehensive staff training and induction program, and the influence of the professional banking skills and knowledge of the new top management.

Diffusion of a culture of performance and accountability

As indicated in the preceding subsections, the review undertaken by the task force necessitated organisational restructuring with the aim of diffusing a culture of performance and accountability. To this end, the task force (with the assistance of the external consultants) developed a vision, mission, and goals, to provide meaningful direction to the management to develop the bank's new strategy (see Table 6.3). Prior to 2000, FUB did not have any explicitly stated vision,

Table 6.3 Vision, mission, and goals of FUB

1	Vision:	To be recognised as a leader and a brand synonymous with trust, highest standards of service quality, international best practices, and social responsibility.
2	Mission:	[FUB]bank will aspire to the values that make [FUB]bank the nation's bank by:

- Institutionalising a merit and performance culture
- Creating a distinctive brand identity by providing the highest standards of service
- Adopting the best international management practices
- Maximising stakeholders' value
- Discharging our responsibility as a good corporate citizen of Pakistan and in countries where we operate

3	Goals:	To enhance profitability and maximisation of [FUB]bank share through increasing leverage of existing customer base and diversified range of products.

Source: FUB (2000)

mission, and goals. A careful examination of the new vision, mission, and goals indicates that they are consistent with the requirements set out in the corporate governance principles issued by the regulators. They are also closely connected and directly related to the new business strategy of the bank. FUB's core values are now depicted within the vision, mission, and goals.[14]

A participant (Business Group Head 7) observed that the management of FUB made an effort to establish a culture of performance and accountability through emphasising the principles presented in the core values of the bank. Management facilitated the institutionalisation of core values by formally communicating them to employees through internal bulletins (e.g., monthly newsletters) and presentations (e.g., training programs and quarterly business meetings of managers). When core values become highly institutionalised, they function as myths that bind organisational systems, procedures, and actions (Scott, 1992). DiMaggio and Powell (1983) identify the role of managers as facilitating the institutionalisation of core values as a key source of normative isomorphic pressure, a pressure which helps in promoting a culture of performance and accountability.

To diffuse the culture of performance and accountability the new top management also introduced a comprehensive employee development and hiring program aimed at middle and lower management levels. The bank invested in developing these managers through need-based training. A participant from a branch (Branch Manger 1) revealed that most of them had a background of working in foreign banks operating in Pakistan, and hence, formed a culture of their own quite different from the managers who were working within the bank prior to 1997. Regional Manager 2 expressed similar views in this regard. He also observed that the new managers were expected to play an important role in adapting FUB's PMS. Since these managers had a common set of values and attitudes, they viewed anticipated change within the bank in a similarly positive fashion. DiMaggio and Powell (1983) describe such values and attitudes as a source of normative isomorphism which occurs through *"filtering of personnel"*. They explicitly state that:

> Within many organizational fields filtering occurs through the hiring of individuals from firms within the same industry; through the recruitment of fast track staff from a narrow range of training institutions; through common promotion practices, such as always hiring top executives from financial or legal departments; and from skill-level requirements for particular job.
>
> (DiMaggio and Powell, 1983, p. 152)

The influence of banking knowledge and skills of the new top management

According to DiMaggio and Powell (1983), normative pressure also stems from and is rooted in the knowledge, skills, and educational background of the organisational members. In the case of FUB, the newly appointed and trained managers required the ability to mobilise the available resources and an understanding of organisational conditions and their environment, and to be attuned to the new situations that might arise after the PMS change. The new President, in this context, played a significant role as the "change agent", as described by Rogers and Shoemaker (1971).[15] For instance, he communicated effectively the need to change the PMS within the bank, thereby gaining the staff's acceptance. At the same time, he established an information flow by placing performance measurement on the agenda of the Management Committee meetings. He drew on his previous banking experience, skills, and knowledge working in a foreign bank to shape and promote changes in the new PMS within FUB.

The President and the Management Committee met monthly to plan the training for relevant staff, and served as the hub of performance measurement communications. To increase the visibility of the PMS change, minutes of these meetings were circulated to business unit managers. It is apparent that the President played a critical role as a change agent in the PMS change. Hence, the research found the new President was a very influential source of normative pressure to change the PMS and was also fundamental in creating the momentum for change. This was supported in the survey, with eleven of the twelve respondents identifying the role of the new President as vital not only in introducing changes in the PMS but also in creating momentum and facilitating the PMS change process. Interpreting his actions in terms of the conceptualisation of DiMaggio and Powell (1983), he played a key role in legitimising the change in the PMS and was able to change the bank's 'public sector' perception among its stakeholders. The foregoing discussion also infers that an essential task of leaders is to pay careful attention to the possible reaction to the PMS change. By meeting this challenge, managers can avoid resistance to change. It appears that the new President was able to gain commitment from employees by highlighting the deficiencies of the old PMS, and convincing them that the new system offered a better and more equitable basis for measuring performance.

6.4　The changes to the PMS in 2000

A new PMS was introduced in 2000 by the task force by way of a circular issued by the newly established Performance Measurement and Budgeting Department. The new PMS was called the "Key Performance Indicators (KPIs) system". Under this system, overall strategic direction was provided by the Board of Directors, and action plans were developed at the branch level and moved up to the regions and to the business groups to ensure ownership and commitment at all levels of the management hierarchy. Following the introduction of the new PMS, the task force was abolished and all responsibilities for coordinating the performance measurement function within the bank were delegated to the Performance Measurement and Budgeting Department.

In contrast to the previous PMS, the emphasis of the new system was on the participation by each management level in the new performance measurement process. The new PMS primarily included three key changes: (i) a new strategic planning and performance measurement process; (ii) changes to the performance measures in use; and (iii) the introduction of a branch profitability report. These changes are described in subsections 6.4.1, 6.4.2 and 6.4.3 respectively.

6.4.1　*A new strategic planning and performance measurement process*

The existing literature shows that the strategic planning process provides the framework from which performance measurement should be developed if the organisation's objectives are to be achieved (Anthony and Govindarajan, 2001). The changes in organisational structure which resulted in the delegation of decision-making authority and responsibilities down to the middle and lower management levels necessitated the proper development of a meaningful strategic planning and performance measurement process. Hence, the bank introduced a new strategic planning and performance measurement process (see Figure 6.3), which began in August each year with a meeting of the Management Committee. The Management Committee reviewed the prior year's operating and financial performance of all business units and identified key strategies that would keep FUB competitive. During the Management Committee meeting, information was presented by various business groups to provide insights into the businesses, products and services, customers, employees, operational difficulties and the effect of new regulations.

By mid-September, the following year's business plan and KPIs were agreed amongst the business group heads and the Management Committee at its quarterly meeting. The business plan outlines the targets, KPIs, and future goals of each business unit and identifies the resources necessary to support their business activities. A participant for a regional office explained that the discussions between the Management Committee and the business group heads helped to ensure that appropriate goals that were measurable were chosen. The business plan trickles down throughout the entire bank from the business groups to the regional offices by way of a circular from the Performance Measurement and Budgeting

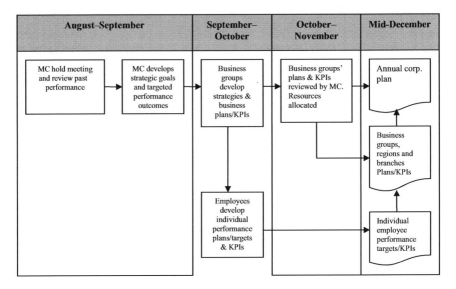

Figure 6.3 Strategic planning and performance measurement process
Source: FUB (2000)

Department. Regional offices then disseminate the business plan to their respective branches. The participants of the research felt that through this process the bank established the legitimacy of those business plans because the bank managers were given ample opportunity to provide feedback. Finally, employees within branches develop their individual KPIs so as to be aligned with the KPIs of their business unit. At the individual employee level, the setting of KPIs and targets is entirely up to the branch manager or head of the department at corporate or regional office. The Management Committee then approves the goals and KPIs by the end of October and budgetary resources are separately allocated based on priorities established by the Board of Directors. Actual performance is then measured on a quarterly basis and compared to the approved goals and KPIs.

Documentary evidence suggests that the new strategic planning and performance measurement process had been a central focus of FUB's efforts to improve its PMS. Additionally, several participants of the research indicated that with the implementation of the new strategic planning and performance measurement process, business units felt that they could control their own activities by setting their own goals and KPIs. A regional manager (Regional Manager 2) viewed the new strategic planning and performance measurement process as a foundation for the new PMS and all twelve of the respondents to the questionnaire indicated that the new strategic planning and performance measurement process influenced the changes in the performance measures used to a great extent. Regional Manager 2 also indicated that the use of this strategic planning and performance measurement process enabled them to capture a comprehensive view of FUB's business activities, thus improving their ability to adopt the performance measurement function more effectively.

With the new President's personal commitment and support, the bank embraced the strategic planning and performance measurement process and made it an integral part of FUB's systems and procedures within a year. In the words of a regional manager, the "new strategic planning and performance measurement process injected a performance culture into the bank . . . not as mere words, but as a key pillar of performance measurement that had produced tangible results for the bank in main functional areas" (Regional Manager 2).

6.4.2 The changes in the performance measures

In contrast to the previous PMS, the bank introduced separate measures for business units, with the number of measures increasing from eleven to twenty-three for the business units at the corporate office level and twenty-one for the regional offices and branches. As described in preceding sections, the changes in the performance measures were required to accommodate new regulatory requirements and the new organisational structure and strategy. A comparative position of the performance measures prior to and during 2000 is shown in Table 6.4.

The new PMS did not adopt any of the measures used prior to 2000. Out of the twenty-three measures introduced, six measures (total advances, private sector advances, public sector advances, advances to government, advances to other banks, and total stuck-up advances within each category of advances) were developed in order to comply with the requirements of the regulators to improve loan portfolio quality. As indicated earlier, in 1997 the regulators directed the banks to classify their non-performing loans into four categories. Banks were also instructed to report, on a quarterly basis, the performance against recovery of non-performing loans for each of these categories together with strategies to improve future recovery processes (State Bank of Pakistan, 1997).

The remaining seventeen performance measures were developed by management to improve the operational and financial controls which were crucial following the changes in organisational structure. While presenting their views on these performance measures, several participants indicated that a number of similar performance measures, such as effective loan costs, the ratio of financial efficiency, net interest rate margin, and risk-weighted capital ratio, were being used by foreign banks in Pakistan. Further discussion with the participants revealed that the new top management overtly promoted these performance measures as they had extensive experience using them in foreign banks prior to joining FUB in 1998. The pressure on the new top management to mimic performance measures used by foreign banks could be seen as an effort to gain legitimacy in the face of the uncertain banking environment (DiMaggio and Powell, 1983). Many of the participants of the research expressed the view that FUB adopted performance measures similar to foreign banks because they had been using them for many years and these banks were considered as highly successful in terms of their operating activities and profitability. A participant, in this regard pointed out that:

> new management was very supportive of using practices similar to the foreign banks . . . I think there could be two reasons for this. They had a long experience of using these measures in the past and were comfortable with

Table 6.4 A comparative position of performance measurement system used in FUB

Prior to 2000	2000	2003 and beyond
1 Average Deposit	1 Interest/Return on Deposit	**Assets Quality:**
2 Foreign Currency Deposits	2 Total Staff Cost	1 Overdue (non-performing) Loans/Total Loans[£]
3 Non-Fund Bases Income	3 Total Operating Cost	2 Loans provisions/Overdue (non-performing) loans
4 Net Performing Advances	4 Income on Liquid Funds	3 Loans provisions/Total loans
5 Non-Performing Loans	5 Interest/Return Income on Advances	4 Total provisions/Total loans
6 Profit/Loss	• Interest paid to branches by H.O.*	5 Doubtful loans/Total loans[£]
7 Advances against Exports	6 Total Commission Exchange and Discount	6 Loss loans/Total loans[£]
8 Advances against Imports	• Other Income	7 Loans to single borrower to net capital[£]
		8 Total realised interest or mark-up/Total interest or mark-up receivable[£]
9 Home Remittances	7 Operating Income	9 Total Loans/Total deposits[£]
10 Cost of Funds	8 Term Deposit Interest Based	10 Total risk-weighted assets/Total assets[£]
11 Intermediate Costs	• Domestic	**Capital Adequacy:**
	• Foreign	11 Regulatory Tier 1 Capital/Total assets
	9 Current Account	12 Regulatory Tier 1 Capital/Risk-weighted assets
	10 Saving Deposit	13 Regulatory Capital/Risk-weighted assets
	11 Term Deposit – PLS	14 Non-Performing loans/Total net capital
	12 Total Deposit	15 Total Capital less non-performing assets/Total risk-weighted assets[£]
	13 Bills and other non-fund business	16 Risk-adjusted return on capital[£]
	14 Cash	**Earning Performance:**
	15 Liquid Funds	17 Total Profit (total net income)/Total capital excluding Reserve (ROE)[£]
	16 Total Advances (amount and percentage)	18 Total Profit (total net income)/Total assets (ROA)[£]
	17 Private sector advances	19 Non-interest or mark-up income/Total income[£]
	Stuck-up advances (amount and percentage)**	20 Non-interest or mark-up expenses/Total income[£]
	18 Public sector advances	21 Other Income/Average Total assets
	• Domestic	22 Other Income/Total income
	• Foreign	23 Gain or loss on foreign exchange activities/Total income[£]
	Stuck-up advances (amount and percentage)**	24 Interest Income less mark-up or interest expense/Total assets[£]

19 Advances to Government

   Stuck-up advances (amount and percentage)**
20 Advances to banks
   • Domestic
   • Foreign
   Stuck-up advances (amount and percentage)**
21 Total stuck-up advances (amount and percentage)**
22 Service-statement of accounts sent by all branches to the clients*
23 Number of Employees

25 Average net interest or mark-up margin of new transactions$^{£}$
26 Gain or losses on securities sales/Total income$^{£}$
   Liquidity Capacity:
27 Deposits with SBP plus cash balances with other banks$^{£}$
28 Liquid assets/Total assets
29 Liquid assets/Liquid liabilities$^{£}$
30 Financial assets portfolio/Total assets
31 Total loans/Total deposits$^{£}$
32 Total loans/Total assets
33 Total money market takings/Total deposits$^{£}$
34 Total money market placements/Total deposits$^{£}$
35 Total loans longer than 1 year/Total assets$^{£}$
36 Total deposits longer than 1 year/Total assets$^{£}$
37 Total loans longer than 3 years/Total assets
38 Total deposits longer than 3 years/Total assets
39 Total government deposits /Total assets
40 Total government deposits years/Total deposits
   General Measures:
41 Loans to Private Sector/Private Sector Deposits
42 Loans to Private Sector/Total loans
43 Domestic loans/Total deposits
44 Total FC assets/Total FC liabilities
45 Growth Rate of Total assets
46 Growth Rate of Total deposits
47 Growth Rate of Total loan facilities

*These measures were not applied in overseas and regional offices.

**The term 'Stuck-up advances' was commonly used in 2000 and referred to as 'non-performing loans'.

$^{£}$These performance measures were designed to accommodate the regulatory requirements in compliance with the CAMELS Framework.

these measures . . . to me this was quite natural. They always talked about the control mechanisms of foreign banks in all our meeting . . . in the late 1990s foreign banks were considered as model institutions for local banks because of their strong liquidity and profitability.

(Regional Manager 2)

The participants' comments reveal that FUB had no option but to develop performance measures similar to foreign banks due to the perceived usefulness of those measures for decision making. The use of such performance measures was relatively new for domestic banks in Pakistan, particularly state-owned banks. While foreign banks' size and operations were to a certain extent different, their systems were cited by the regulators as the best prototype, as revealed by Branch Manager 2, who said:

although foreign banks in Pakistan were small in size they were very strategic in managing their activities . . . they were mainly concentrating on international trade and foreign exchange related business. . . . They had very strong internal controls . . . in the several quarterly meetings of the State Bank of Pakistan with the Presidents of banks, they [State Bank of Pakistan] always encouraged [us] to use similar types of systems and processes in the local banks.

This type of response by FUB can be seen as acquiescence to the accepted performance measurement practice in terms of Oliver's (1991) framework. This finding is consistent with the explanation of Oliver (1991, p. 146) who suggests that organisations either consciously or unconsciously mimic organisational models, including, for example, "the imitation of successful organizations and the acceptance of advice from consulting firms or professional associations" (p. 152). This view is also illustrative of the fact that FUB copied other banks in order to gain competitive advantage.

6.4.3 The introduction of a branch profitability report

As noted earlier, in addition to increasing the number of performance measures, an important development of the revised PMS was the introduction of a "branch profitability" report (see Table 6.5). The branch profitability report focused on three elements: the income from interest, foreign exchange and commissions; the expenses and cost of deposits; and a summary of deposits at a given point in time. The report was used to analyse profitability by account (product) type and customer groups in relation to each branch at regional level. Studies in this area have shown that banks who intend to increase profitability focus more on financial measures and adopt sophisticated financial methods such as profitability reporting (e.g., Helliar et al., 2002). By the beginning of each quarter, the Performance Measurement and Budgeting Department presented the consolidated performance reports together with the profitability reports to the Management

Table 6.5 Branch profitability report

Total Income	Amount (previous)	% of Income	Amount (current)	% of Income
Interest Earned:				
• Financing				
• Cash Finance				
• Demand Finance				
• Running Finance				
• Funds Lent to H.O.				
Exchange Income:				
• Remittance				
• Foreign Exchange				
• Bills Purchased				
Commissions:				
• Bills				
• Foreign Exchange				
• Govt A/C				
Discount				
Total Expenses				
Profit Paid:				
• Term Deposit				
• Saving Deposits				
• Funds from H.O.				
Other Expenses:				
• Personnel				
• Total Others				
Branch Profit/Loss				

Deposits:	No. of A/Cs	% of Total	Amount	% of Total
• Term Account				
• Saving Accounts				
• Current Accounts				
Total				
Cost of Deposits:				
• Profit on Deposits as a percentage of total deposits				
Cost of Profit Bearing Deposits:				
• Profit on Deposits as a percentage of F.D. and S.B.				
Officer Productivity:				
• Deposits divided by the number of the officers				
Total Staff Productivity:				
• Deposits divided by total number of staff				

F.D. Accounts:	Number	% of Total	Deposits	% of Total
• Large (top 20%)				
• Medium (Middle 20%)				
• Small (Lower 20%)				
S.B. Accounts:				
• Large (top 20%)				
• Medium (Middle 20%)				
• Small (Lower 20%)				
Current Accounts:				
• Large (top 20%)				
• Medium (Middle 20%)				
• Small (Lower 20%)				

Source: FUB (2000, Performance Measurement Manual)

Committee. These reports were then discussed in the meeting to assess the performance of each business unit against overall targets and KPIs. The relevant abstracts of the minutes of these meetings were then circulated to the concerned business units to take the actions suggested by the Management Committee.

A number of participants, in particular, Branch Manager 1, revealed that the introduction of the branch profitability report created some discomfort and unease amongst the branch managers as they believed that its introduction would result in the closure of branches situated in rural areas where business potential was very low, and result in layoffs. They also expected an increase in their work load. For example, under the change, branch managers needed to provide the related data monthly, and given that some of this data was produced manually, it was time consuming and cumbersome. The lack of technical support and training for employees at branches also led to frustration, as revealed by a participant:

> We experienced difficulties because the training and support provided was not adequate. Many branch managers lost interest in these reports because data compilation was tedious . . . technical approvals and hardware and software support from the head office was not timely available.
>
> (Branch Manager 1)

6.5 Pressure to change the PMS: 2000–2003

In this section the nature of pressures that influenced FUB to change its PMS after 2000 are discussed. These pressures are discussed in subsections 6.5.1 and 6.5.2 respectively.

6.5.1 Pressure from regulators

During the period 2000–2002, coercive pressure was again instrumental in influencing changes to FUB's PMS. These coercive pressures mainly resulted from regulatory changes, in particular, the adoption of IFRSs and the CAMELS Framework. In 2000, the regulators instructed banks to adopt IFRSs (IFRSs 21, 32, 39, and 40) and International Audit Standards, and comply with standardised reporting systems including certain disclosure requirements (see Table 5.1). According to a participant (Business Group Head 1), compliance with these standards was crucial to increase the credibility of the financial statements as well as to improve transparency. As mentioned earlier in Chapter 3, such conformity has been shown by institutional theorists such as DiMaggio and Powell (1983) to be a way to secure legitimacy from the regulatory authorities and the general public.

The PMS was affected by the adoption of the IFRSs because its disclosure requirements specify that management must report the financial risks of the bank and how the bank intended to manage such risks. This required a PMS that captured risk-adjusted performance measures. Most of the participants interviewed believed that the software developed for the PMS in 2000 was not suited to measuring risk-adjusted performance. Consequently, FUB needed to align its PMS based on a different set of risk-adjusted performance measures, one that would be used by the bank to report its performance.

As noted in Chapter 5, at the end of 2002 the regulators implemented the CAMELS Framework to monitor the performance of banks operating in Pakistan. The framework required FUB to provide information on six groups of performance measures. These performance measures included: Capital Adequacy (e.g., capital to risk-weighted assets ratio); Asset Quality (e.g., non-performing loans to advances, loan default to total advances, and recoveries to loan default ratios); Management Soundness (e.g., ability to plan and react to changing circumstances, technical competence, leadership and administrative ability); Earnings and Profitability (e.g., return on Assets); Liquidity (e.g., gap between rate sensitive assets and rate sensitive liabilities and liquid to total assets ratio); and Sensitivity to Market risk (e.g., management's ability to monitor and control a bank's exposure to interest rate risk, foreign exchange volatility, and equity price risks). All of the participants of the research believed that the need to provide performance information on the basis of the CAMELS Framework represented a major change within the banking sector. This change coerced FUB to review the compatibility of its performance measures with the CAMELS Framework requirements. This review remained on FUB's agenda for several months thereafter.

A careful examination of the requirements under the CAMELS Framework (see Table 5.3) highlights that the performance measures recommended under this framework were risk-adjusted and different from the ones developed by FUB in 2000. For this reason, the lack of compatibility of the PMS developed in 2000 with the new requirements under the CAMELS Framework was a major concern. Hence, in order to meet the regulators' requirements, the Performance Measurement and Budgeting Department coerced the business units to submit two separate performance measurement reports every quarter end i.e., a report under the existing PMS for the Management Committee meetings and a new report, on an interim basis, to supply information to the regulators. The report for the regulators was to be in line with the requirements of the Basel Accord conditions (State Bank of Pakistan, 2002).

Two participants (Regional Manager 1 and Branch Manager 2) specifically noted that the reports for the regulators required more specific and focused performance information than before. In addition, Regional Manager 1 said that the need to provide performance information on the basis of the CAMELS Frameworks coerced FUB to introduce new performance measures in line with the requirements of the regulators. FUB had no alternative but to comply with the requirements of these new regulations, with failure to comply with these regulations inviting "the risk of legal or regulatory sanctions, financial loss, or loss to reputation the bank may suffer as a result of its failure to comply with all applicable laws, regulations, codes of conduct and standards of good practices" (FUB, 2004, p. 3). Thus, "compliance" was the only response available to FUB (Oliver, 1991).

6.5.2 Operational difficulties with the PMS developed in 2000

A number of participants noted certain operational difficulties following the implementation of the PMS developed in 2000. For instance, a participant from a branch (Branch Manager 1) indicated that although this system was quite comprehensive and involved a rigorous strategic planning and performance measurement process, managers had difficulty in using it due to the inadequate information provided by the system. Another branch manager stated:

> There were times when we used the system [Performance Measurement] more intensively; however, at times, management lost interest in measuring performance as other priorities prevailed because the business and economic situation in Pakistan was so tense. Staff failed to provide timely and the latest information.
>
> (Branch Manager 2)

Branch Manager 1 also observed that a large share of the data had to be calculated and entered in the spreadsheets. These spreadsheets, using a stand-alone software application, were maintained independently by the business units to manage clusters of data from different processes. Most of the participants recalled that the main weaknesses associated with the use of the spreadsheets included: the lack of an integrated approach to measure and report key performance and risk information; the lack of data security; and the provision of out-of-date information. Further, another participant (Regional Manager 2) revealed that the Performance Measurement and Budgeting Department's staff had to collect information from over 1,500 branches and prepare relevant performance measurement reports manually. While these reports were deemed to be for the purpose of measuring the performance of the business activities, the information supplied was frequently unreliable. This in turn reduced the usefulness of the performance reports.

Discussion with the participants indicated that they required a system which not only provided accurate and timely information, but also provided a comprehensive view of each business activity's economic and risk-adjusted value. The following comments by a branch manager and business group head reflect the importance of providing timely information:

> by providing appropriate and well-timed information to business heads with risk based performance reports, they can develop quick win strategies to improve the contribution of each business activity, optimise customer service, raise asset quality and profitability.
>
> (Branch Manager 1)

> to survive in a tougher financial market we need to ensure that we deliver products and services that customers recognize. In order to improve our service model, we needed information from multiple sources, timely produced with improved transparency. This could be done through implementing an integrated performance measurement framework with full automation and online facilities.
>
> (Business Group Head 5)

The participants of the research also voiced their concerns in regard to the bank's communication network. In particular, they indicated that top management experienced a high level of anxiety due to delays in receiving information from the branches relating to decisions concerning deposits and investments at the corporate office. This caused further administrative work and required follow-ups to collect information from branches. This problem is reflected in the following comments:

> Staff in branch voiced that they were overloaded with various tasks . . . they were unable to reconcile accounts promptly and always delayed in despatching branch performance position to the head office important decisions.
>
> (Regional Manager 2)

> the information revived from the field was always outdated and delayed despite the fact that we set tight timelines for the information. Repeatedly the information received was inaccurate. Many problems that surfaced had to be managed through temporary solutions. Regional chiefs were not aware of the performance of the branch under their control.
>
> (Business Group Head 4)

The responses suggest that the coercive pressure emanating from the regulator's new directives to adopt risk-adjusted performance measures under the CAMELS Framework, and the operational difficulties with the existing PMS, triggered a new series of performance measurement discussions in the bank. Such a response was necessary for FUB to retain its legitimacy and support from the regulators.

The President and the Management Committee invited the business unit managers to participate in a series of meetings in late 2002 and early 2003. These meetings were coordinated by the Performance Measurement and Budgeting Department. The discussions led to subsequent changes to the PMS, including the complete automation and integration of the performance measurement function, with advanced features to assess risk-adjusted values.

6.6 The changes to the PMS in 2003 and beyond

Beginning in 2003, FUB decided to replace the spreadsheets and adopt Enterprise resource planning (ERP) standard software based on the Oracle database platform. This system enabled FUB to enhance the capabilities of its PMS and to monitor key performance information in real time. The strategic planning and performance measurement process implemented in 2000 was left unchanged. However, the branch profitability report was discontinued and replaced with a more comprehensive branch balance sheet and income statement.

The new PMS, as claimed by a participant from the branch (Branch Manager 1) provided "enhanced features that enabled [Pak]bank to incorporate a broad range of new measures for each business area and functional hierarchy". Additionally, the PMS incorporated Oracle's internal fund transfer pricing, cost allocations, and activity-based profitability analysis tools to support performance measurement. Furthermore, several participants revealed that the Oracle PMS enabled FUB to calculate the risk of each account held at the bank and then aggregate these risks by customer, product, and market segment. This was a step forward towards developing risk-adjusted performance measures as directed by the regulators. Many participants commented on the benefits of the Oracle database platform. For instance, a branch manager said:

> The shift away from the manual performance measurement work and processes with automation enabled branch employees to exert concerted efforts to other business activities and services, which appeared to be more rewarding for the employees. The system facilitated us to develop a customer profile system which made it possible for us to compete more effectively in terms of customer service, cross selling and development of innovative products and services.
>
> (Branch Manager 1)

While the regulators applied coercive pressures to adopt risk-adjusted performance measures, the decision to automate the performance measurement function was purely management's own initiative in an attempt to enhance efficiency and internal controls. In this regard, the response of the bank can be categorised as a balancing tactic, used to demonstrate a commitment to compliance while achieving efficiency-related motives (e.g., Tsamenyi et al., 2006; Siti-Nabiha and Scapens, 2005). The balancing tactic enabled FUB to serve their interest more effectively by obtaining an acceptable compromise between internal objectives and institutional expectations under the new regulations (Oliver, 1991).

While the Oracle database platform was installed at various business units, the Management Committee began deliberations on the specific performance measures. A participant (Regional Manager 1) pointed out that the discussion in the meetings mainly revolved around what measures to present in the system, how and when the measurement would take place, and who would be responsible for reporting the results. The intention of the Management Committee was to identify performance measures that would enable the business units to provide management with a comprehensive view of their business activities. Simultaneously, the PMS also had to comply with the regulator's directives under the newly adopted CAMELS Framework. Compliance with these regulators' directives was aimed at increasing the credibility of financial statements as well as bringing about greater transparency and increased public disclosure (DiMaggio and Powell, 1983).

6.6.1 Development of new performance measures

The participants of the research revealed that when developing performance measures, interviews were conducted with the representatives of the business groups at corporate and regional offices to gain their insights. This input was sought to find out which performance measures would best describe their performance and facilitate the monitoring of business activities. The intention of management was to identify performance measures that would apply across different business areas and which would offer an additional, synergetic benefit if measured on a more aggregate level. Further, the PMS specifies measures for the categories considered relevant in evaluating performance as well as reporting the operating and financial condition of the bank to the regulators i.e., the measures that pertain to capital adequacy, asset quality, earnings performance, and liquidity capacity.

In June 2003, a performance measurement report which included forty-seven performance measures was developed (see Table 6.4). This report included twenty-four measures designed to comply with the requirements of the CAMELS Framework, with a large number of measures subdivided, to display performance from different perspectives. The measure "position of recovery against non-performing loans", for instance, was viewed from a national, regional, and industry perspective. In contrast to the PMS implemented in 2000, in order to track the performance of the field offices, measures were selected to consider the relevance of their business activities. For instance, each region and branch in the system had different market demographics and opportunities. Therefore, each branch had measures that were unique to that branch. Table 6.4 clearly depicts that all forty-seven new performance measures were financial in nature. This contrasts with the literature in relation to manufacturing organisations in developed countries, where substantial changes in the nature and intensity of competition have forced them to pay more attention to a combination of both financial and non-financial measures to make a PMS effective (Ittner and Larcker, 1998, p. 218). A research conducted by CIMA (1993) also reported that manufacturing organisations adopt both financial and non-financial performance measures mainly because they provide the right direction for meeting the recent changes in the manufacturing environment. The participants of the research revealed that since FUB primarily wanted to improve financial performance while complying with the new regulatory requirements, which required using financial measures, the bank emphasised using financial measures alone.

In August 2003, the Management Committee deliberated on the revised system and decided to make further changes due to recent changes in regulatory requirements and the responsibilities assigned to some particular business units. Consequently, some measures were removed completely, some new measures were brought in, and others were simply adjusted in terms of how to measure them. In addition, existing measures that were not clearly defined in regard to measurement or responsibility (e.g., Regulatory Tier 1 Capital) were omitted with the option to reinstate them in the future. Following the approval by the Board of Directors, the Management Committee implemented the new PMS with effect from the financial year commencing July 2004.

Each measure in the report was described as to how and when measurement should take place, and who was responsible for reporting the results. Although most participants argued that the latest measures represented a new strategic direction for the bank, some participants also noted certain limitations in the design of the PMS, primarily in relation to the choice of measures. For instance, a branch manager and a participant from a regional office pointed out that although innovativeness is an important measure in the banking industry, it was not included in the new PMS as it is difficult to identify and measure in state-owned institutions like FUB.

The reports containing information concerning performance results move up through the system: from branch manager, to regional manager, and then to the relevant business group head. The consolidated performance results for each business group are then reported to the Management Committee and the President on a monthly basis for review. The information on these performance results is available in formats based on time periods and business areas.

The participants revealed that the consolidated performance measurement reports were discussed at the quarterly Board meetings together with the targets for the upcoming quarter. According to Business Group Head 5, these meetings contributed to aligning the business units' performance to the overall goals and strategy of the bank. In addition, these meetings ensured the Board of Directors' involvement in the bank's progress which is necessary to ensure that strategies are implemented and goals are achieved (Anthony and Govindarajan, 2001). This is reflected in the following comment of a regional manager:

> in Board meetings in which we discuss performance for each business unit, important decisions are made about what actions we have to take in case of deviations.

(Regional Manager 2)

An examination of internal documents indicated that performance with respect to the strategic plan was tracked for all goals and targets at all levels of the bank. However, the Board only reviewed a specific set of financial measures (see Table 6.6) that reflected results in core performance categories as required by the regulators in the CAMELS Framework. These performance dimensions included: (i) earnings performance; (ii) asset quality; (iii) liquidity capacity; and (iv) capital adequacy. It appears that the Board reviewed these performance measures to discharge the responsibility required of them by the regulators to strengthen internal controls in the bank (State Bank of Pakistan, 2004). This is demonstrated from the State Bank of Pakistan's Directive No. 7 of 2004, which states:

> As a part of our ongoing efforts to improve performance, controls and compliance objectives within banks in Pakistan . . . their Board of Directors are required to ensure existence of an effective system of internal control . . . the internal control system must include a mechanism to review the indicators for assets protection, operational efficiency and risk management . . . the internal control system will be tested/checked by our inspectors and will factor in the CAMELS-S rating system under 'S' (Systems & Controls).

(State Bank of Pakistan, 2004)

Table 6.6 Performance measures reported to the Board of Directors

Area of assessment	Key performance indicators
1 **Earnings performance**	• Total profit (total net income)/Total assets (ROA) • Total profit (total net income)/Total capital excluding reserves (ROE) • Non-interest or mark-up income/Total income • Non-interest or mark-up expenses/Total income • Average net interest or mark-up margins of new transactions • Gains or losses on securities sales/Total income • Gains or losses on foreign exchange activities/Total income • Interest income less mark-up or interest expense/Total assets
2 **Asset quality**	• Overdue (non-performing) loans/Total loans • Doubtful loans/Total loans • Loss loans/Total loans • Loans to single borrower to net capital • Total realised interest or mark-up/Total interest/ mark-up receivable • Total loans/Total deposits • Total risk-weighted assets/Total assets
3 **Liquidity capacity**	• Deposits with SBP plus cash balance • Total money market takings/Total deposits • Total money market placements/Total deposits • Liquid assets/Liquid liabilities • Total loans longer than 1 year/Total assets • Total deposits longer than 1 year/Total assets • Total loans/Total assets
4 **Capital adequacy**	• Total capital less non-performing assets/Total risk-weighted assets • Risk-adjusted return on capital

According to a number of participants, the new PMS enabled business unit managers to improve the bank's internal controls and also to improve their ability to comply with the central bank's regulations. This is substantiated by the following view expressed by FUB's President and published in the preamble of the Directors' Report of the Annual Report (FUB, 2005, p. 20):

> Bank's management has established and is maintaining an adequate and effective system . . . which encompasses the policies, procedures, processes, and tasks as approved by the Board of Directors that facilitate effective and efficient operations. The management and the employees at all levels within the Bank are required to perform as per . . . control system components. The . . . system ensures quality of external and internal reporting, maintenance of proper records and processes, compliance with applicable laws and regulations and internal policies with respect to conduct of business.

6.6.2 Implementation of the new performance measurement system

Although the new PMS was implemented in July 2004, the system was initially implemented at only the corporate level, with the regional offices and branches still using the old spreadsheet system which was then collated and entered into the central system manually. This continued to frustrate the employees working in these branches/business units. The PMS was designed and built by the new business group heads without any major input from the first-line managers of various business units, including branch managers, as to what information and KPIs needed to be included in the system. Further, due to the partial computerisation at the initial stage, data was entered manually into the PMS by most of the branches, which delayed the entire process and caused a great deal of frustration amongst the users of PMS, especially branch managers. Hence, during 2005 the database was further adapted to suit the needs of each individual business unit/branch. The centralised and fully integrated PMS was implemented at all levels of the bank, including regional offices and branches, by mid-2005.

The PMS implemented in July 2004 was being used by the bank at the time of collecting data for this research (i.e., January 2008). A few participants indicated that they were considering adopting a Balanced Scorecard in the near future. However, the decision to develop and implement a Balanced Scorecard had not materialised when data was collected. This finding is consistent with several management accounting studies from emerging economies. For instance, Waweru et al. (2004) suggest that the use of multidimensional PMSs are not very common in developing countries unlike developed countries where the use of multidimensional measures are very common and have existed for a long time. A participant, in this regard stated that:

> The employees are being trained at regular intervals so that it keeps abreast of new banking techniques and external trends . . . we have established a strong performance culture and now we are seriously considering a proposal to adopt a Balanced Scorecard which is being used by many foreign banks' branches.
>
> (Branch Manager 2)

Table 6.7 presents a summary of the key features of the PMS being used prior to 1997 and the PMSs developed in 2000 and 2003. These features depict that with the change in the PMS in 2000 and again in 2003, not only did the number of performance measures used in FUB increase, but their use had also become more visible throughout the bank. According to the participants, the new PMS was increasingly and extensively used following its implementation in 2004 with the changes in the system perceived to be extremely useful for improving efficiency, performance, and accountability within the bank. This feedback suggests that the new PMS was perceived as being institutionalised within FUB. Employees had a clear understanding of the changes in the external environment (in particular regulatory changes and increased competition) and what needed to be done at

Table 6.7 Key features of the performance measurement system

Feature of the PMS	Prior to 2000	2000	2003 and beyond
Number of measures	11	23	47
Frequency of performance measurement	Yearly	Quarterly	Monthly (continuous)
Measurement process	Centralised at Corporate office	Participative at all levels, i.e., corporate office, regions, and branches	Participative at all levels, i.e., corporate office, regions, and branches
Measures linked to vision and strategy	No	Yes	Yes
Purpose and use	Limited use in planning, decision making, and control	Extensive use in planning, decision making, and control	Extensive use in planning, decision making, and control
Focus of measurement	Financial	Financial and operational efficiency and effectiveness	Financial and operational efficiency and effectiveness
Integration with other management systems	No	Yes	Yes
Type of technology used for performance measurement function	Spreadsheets	Spreadsheets	ERP Oracle Database

the organisational level (adapting the organisational structure and the PMS in line with external environment changes). Overall, the PMS change seems to have enabled the performance measurement function to be more embedded in the norms and habits within the bank.

6.7 Employees' reactions to the PMS changes in 2000 and 2003

Change is often associated with resistance due to conflicts between the norms and values implied by new and existing systems within an organisation.[16] For instance, a new PMS can be perceived by employees to contradict the existing organisational norms and values. If the change is not congruent with these norms and values, it will be resisted, with the intensity of such resistance depending on organisational factors such as leadership and culture, which either support or constrain the change (Hannan, 2005). In FUB, there was evidence of dissatisfaction by employees to the changes to the PMS in 2000 and 2003. However, evidence of dissatisfaction to change in the PMS was minimal. Several participants of the research indicated that employees were reluctant to voice objections to the changes in the system openly because of the potentially negative effects on their employment at the bank. This is not surprising given the culture, norms, and values of the organisations in emerging economies where employees are reluctant to formally and openly criticise organisational policies and management practices (Waweru et al., 2004; Chow et al., 1999; Uddin and Hopper, 1999; Alam, 1997).

There were several reasons for employees' dissatisfaction with the changes to the PMS. According to a number of participants, under the new PMS, employees experienced difficulties in translating their activities into KPIs and setting targets for these KPIs. This, as remarked by Branch Manager 1, resulted in some discomfort amongst the more experienced employees of the bank who had been working in the bank long before the organisational change initiatives in 1997. Employees also perceived the PMS as a top management imposition that would create redundancies and relocation. Moreover, according to a number of participants, under the old PMS system, promotions of employees and their bonuses and salary increments were based on years of experience at FUB rather than performance based and, hence, there was no motivation for them to alter their performance level. Their initial understanding of the new PMS as a performance reporting tool instead of as a strategic management tool created further negative sentiments about the PMS change. The lack of appropriate communication of the new system (for instance through internal office memos and circulars) to the relevant managers appears to be the likely reason for this. A branch manager in this context commented:

> Yes, managers felt that they are not going to get annual bonuses . . . [the] new system stressed performance based rewards and promotions. . . . We thought the system is developed to produce a few reports for the management.
>
> (Branch Manager 1)

Several participants also revealed that although management provided technical support and arranged training programs for employees, the limited frequency of these training programs and deficiencies in the technical support led to further frustration. This finding is similar to Kasurinen (2002), who argued that the absence of technical support largely affects employees' work commitment and their support of changes. Several participants indicated that the change also caused uncertainty amongst some employees due to their inability to understand the reason for changing the previous system. Most of the participants recalled several change initiatives in the past and their subsequent abandonment after only a short period due to frequent changes in the top management by the government. For example, the change initiated in 1989 failed to produce the intended results and consequently employees lost confidence in any changes subsequently proposed within the bank. As a result, employees were indecisive about how seriously they should take the new changes, and whether it was really worth investing their time and effort in their implementation.

While investigating the intensity of employees' reaction to PMS change, it was clear that their resistance neither interrupted the operations of the bank nor delayed the implementation of the changes in the PMS. Most concerns were raised by the employees in informal meetings and briefings to staff concerning changes to the PMS. As remarked by a Business Group Head:

> I don't recall any complaint officially recorded by any individual manager or group of managers . . . even by our employees' union and officers' association. . . . Yes, on certain occasions some managers expressed their feelings and doubts about the change.
>
> (Business Group Head 6)

Several studies argue that improving employee commitment requires communicating a rationale for change to employees, their participation and involvement in the change process, facilitation and support from top management, and providing employees a sense of security (McColl-Kennedy and Anderson, 2005). In FUB, in order to minimise employees' dissatisfaction and resistance to change, a participant from the regional office (Regional Manager 1) revealed that management organised workshops throughout the change process to disseminate and explain changes in the PMS. The new President played an important role in motivating employees and convincing them of the increased effectiveness and efficiency of the new system. As noted in the earlier discussions in this chapter, the new President was characterised as a "change agent". Modell (2007) argues that in addition to top management support, the commitment and active support of the middle and lower level managers is also needed in order for change to happen. In his endeavour to introduce change, the new President was assisted by the new group heads who were assigned the responsibility of implementing the new PMS. The group heads exchanged ideas with the President and communicated those ideas to the first-line managers through formal and informal meetings. Hence, as described by Rogers (1995), they performed the role of "opinion leaders", i.e., individuals who can informally influence employee behaviour and attitudes in a desired way for creating acceptance of changes. They facilitated the PMS change because they spent a considerable amount of time and effort developing the new system to fit FUB's needs and also assisted with training other employees in the workings of the system which eventually helped in the successful implementation of the new PMS. They also discussed with employees potential improvements in the integration of the PMS.

Consistent with the finding of Cobb et al. (1995), the new group heads' role as opinion leaders appears to have been extremely helpful in understanding and communicating the PMS change. Such a role was used to institutionalise the changes among the employees. These views are consistent with Kotter and Schlesinger (1979), who suggest that employees need to be informed about the change, in particular its consequences, in order to create their commitment and to minimise resistance. More generally, the findings are also consistent with Kasurinen (2002) who suggests that internal commitment is necessary to drive the employees in the successful implementation of change. In FUB, the new group heads introduced the major change in the PMS in 2000. They also constantly advocated the need to change the system and participated actively in formal and informal discussions concerning performance measurement. The fact that most of these staff were involved in the implementation would have also been a contributing factor as to why the change took place without strong resistance. Specifically, when employees understand the need for change, and its consequences and benefits, they are more likely to accept it (Oliver, 1991).

Many participants stated that when employees recognised the benefits of using the new system, they were much more amenable to the changes. A participant from a regional office added:

> There were some technical issues at the beginning of the change . . . most of the staff felt the change is being introduced to further downsize the staff . . . but they [management] were very proactive in providing training and communicating with the staff.
>
> We are quite satisfied. Most of the employees within the bank are satisfied as the new system helped in improving bank's performance and the new performance measurement system is delivering whatever was expected from the change.
>
> (Regional Manager 1)

The management accounting literature suggests that when employees expect benefits, they are likely to develop greater commitment to PMS change and that a proposed change would be more readily accepted if it pledges positive results (Siti-Nabiha and Scapens, 2005). Several participants of the research believed that as a result of the commitment of top management, FUB was able to exercise more control over business activities and improve performance. This was exhibited in the increased profits of the bank to $202.4 million in 2004 and $432.1 million in 2007. The following statement made by the President of FUB further supports this claim.

> We had a cost to income of 92 per cent in the year 1999 and now have a cost to income of 43 per cent which is why in terms of return on capital we achieved the highest ranking in Asia.
>
> (*The New York Times*, 2004)

6.8 Summary

This chapter examined changes in relation to the PMS within FUB. In particular, using the analytical framework developed in Chapter 3, the chapter described how FUB's PMS changed, what factors influenced the bank to change its PMS and FUB's responses to the pressures they faced to change its PMS. The findings of the research are summarised in Table 6.8.

Table 6.8 Factors that influenced changes in the performance measurement system and FUB's responses to the pressures

Type of macro-level conditions	Type of pressure	Main source of pressure	Mechanism of isomorphism	Response to pressure
• Economic and political instability • Introduction of financial sector reforms • Increased competition • Increased general public's expectations for accountability and transparency from state-owned banks • Undue interference from the government, political parties, and staff unions in state-owned banks	Coercive pressures	• Central bank's regulations • Board of Directors' directives • New President's instructions	• Coercion Through regulatory changes in Pakistan's banking sector. Directives from the Board of Directors and the new President of the bank to promote efficiency, performance, and accountability.	Strategy: • Acquiescence tactic: • Comply The bank decided to follow the directives of the regulators. They noted the resource dependence relationship with the regulators and the power to enforce the regulations.
	Mimetic pressures	• New top management • Focus of product innovations • Focus on adopting contemporary banking technologies	• Imitation Appointment of a new President and new business group heads and the formation of a task force and the appointment of an external consultant. Well-developed contemporary banking products and innovative banking technologies being used by other private and foreign banks.	Strategy: • Acquiescence tactic: • Imitate The bank imitated the practices of the foreign banks, considered successful by the regulators. Limited domestic public sector banks' options New breed of managers/senior managers having experience working in private/foreign banks.
	Normative pressures	• Filtering of personnel • New top management's banking knowledge and skills • Employees training and induction program	• Professionalisation Through the education and/or training received by organisational members, which enhanced their ability to develop and promote new rules, systems, and routines within the bank. The influence of the professional banking skills and knowledge of the new top management.	Strategy: • Compromise tactic: • Balance Opinion leaders' skills and knowledge. Training of managerial staff pushed to balance compromise and acquiescence strategies.

The analysis revealed that the changes in the PMS took place on two occasions, 2000 and 2003. In 2000, changes in the PMS were introduced in response to the significant changes in FUB's external environment which in turn led to significant regulatory changes in the banking sector. While regulatory changes applied coercive pressure and directly influenced the PMS through the requirements to adopt certain performance measures, other changes in the PMS were introduced in response to changes in FUB's structure and strategy. Coercive pressure was also seen in the form of directives from the Board of Directors and the new President of the bank in an attempt to promote efficiency, performance, and accountability. There was also evidence to suggest that the bank faced mimetic and normative pressures to change the PMS. The mimetic pressure was exerted through the eagerness of FUB to adopt best practices after the appointment of a new President and business group heads, the formation of a task force, and the appointment of an external consultant. The bank also focused on introducing contemporary banking products and technologies.

The normative pressures were generated after the implementation of a staff training program, and through the professionalism of new top management. In response to these pressures the bank introduced three changes to its PMS: (i) they implemented a comprehensive strategic planning and performance measurement process, (ii) a new set of performance measures was introduced replacing the existing eleven performance measures, and (iii) a branch profitability report was required. The bank commenced measuring performance on a quarterly basis as compared to a yearly basis and started using the PMS more extensively for planning and control purposes.

In 2003, the bank again introduced changes to its PMS mainly due to coercive pressures, with the bank having to comply with further regulatory changes during the period 2000–2002. Normative pressures also influenced the PMS, with the banking professionals expressing their dissatisfaction with the technological support provided for the new PMS. This resulted in the replacement of the operating system that formerly supported the performance measurement function within the bank. Following the adoption of the ERP Oracle database system, FUB was able to measure performance on a monthly basis and integrate the PMS with the bank's other associated management systems, such as risk measurement, internal fund transfer pricing, cost allocations, and activity-based profitability analysis tools.

The research provides limited evidence of active strategic responses to the pressures (i.e., efforts to avoid, defy, and manipulate). This is not surprising, given the change in a considerably controlled environment such as the banking sector (DiMaggio and Powell, 1991). Organisations operating in such environments are inclined to select less active strategic responses (Oliver, 1991). This supports the argument that organisations become less active in their individual responses when they operate in a highly coercive environment. Overall, the PMS change within the bank was congruent with the expectations of its environment, more specifically, the regulators, the government, and the wider community.

The chapter also highlighted the strong role of top management in changing the PMS at FUB. They planned, organised, implemented, and oversaw the changes in the PMS. Despite their efforts, there was some degree of dissatisfaction with the change. The resistance to change, though minimal, was more visible amongst branch managers who faced the greatest uncertainty relating to the operational aspects of the changes. The new President and the business group heads managed to minimise the resistance by promoting the benefits of the new PMS, and by providing technical support and training. Hence, top management played an important role in recognising when resistance occurred and clearly communicating the expected benefits of the changes to the PMS. This strategy not only helped top management to improve employee commitment to the change but also helped to institutionalise a performance measurement and accountability culture within the bank.

Notes

1 While FUB commenced its first Islamic banking branch in December 2006, and a further two Islamic branches by the end of 2007, there is no evidence to indicate that the bank developed separate performance measures or performance measurement processes to evaluate the performance of these branches.

2 As noted in Chapter 5, the Pakistan Banking Council (PBC) was formed under the Banks Nationalisation Act (1974) to perform various functions in line with the objectives of nationalisation. The Pakistan Banking Council was abolished in 1997 after the repeal of the Bank Nationalisation Act (1974).

3 The National Credit Consultative Council (NCCC) was formed in 1972 to oversee the flow of credit to the designated targets set for different segments of the economy. The higher share of directed credit by the NCCC resulted in investments by banks with low rate of returns, which subsequently burdened banks with large non-performing loans (State Bank of Pakistan, 2000).

4 It is important to note that non-performing loans not only constrained the earning opportunities of the bank, but also increased the provisions against the non-performing loans, thereby compelling banks to maintain profitability by increasing spread.

5 Higher provisioning against non-performing loans negatively affected the capital base through the profit and loss account, while higher growth in non-performing loans increased the weight of risky assets in the assets portfolio.

6 The memorandums included business unit performance measurement reports, variance reports, and various other documents on performance-related issues.

7 The Management Committee included the heads of all divisions.

8 As described in Chapter 4, every participant of the research was also asked to complete a questionnaire prior to the interview. The responses given in these questionnaires were used to substantiate interview responses.

9 A directive was issued after the promulgation of the Banking Companies (Recovery of loans, advances, audit, and finance) Ordinance 1997 by the Government of Pakistan (State Bank of Pakistan, 2000).

10 Under the requirements of the "Fit and Proper Test" the appointment of members on the Board of Directors and senior executives was subject to fulfilling a five-dimensional criteria, namely (i) Integrity, Honesty, and Reputation; (ii) Track Record; (iii) Solvency and Integrity; (iv) Qualification and Experience; and (v) Conflict of Interest.

11 The new President had extensive experience working in foreign banks operating in Pakistan and abroad.

12 The old divisional heads were divested from important responsibilities and simultaneously they were offered a voluntary separation package. With the joining of

the new group heads, the old divisional heads also relinquished their role in the Management Committee.

13 The regional business chief is responsible for all 'front office' activities and is supported by the other two regional chiefs. The regional operations chief is responsible for all 'back office' activities including compliance, and providing all the logistical and infrastructure support required by the regional offices and branches. The regional risk management chief provides checks on all investments including loans and links risk management and control processes to help protect the bank's assets.

14 The core values included: highest standard of integrity; institutionalising a teamwork and performance culture; excellence in service; advancement in skills for tomorrow's challenges; awareness of social and community responsibility; and value creation for all stakeholders.

15 According to Rogers and Shoemaker (1971, pp. 229–230), the change agent's attributes include: "1) developing/identifying a need for change; 2) establishing an information exchange relationship; 3) diagnosing potential adopter problems; 4) creating intent to change in the adopters; 5) translating intent into action; 6) stabilizing adoption and preventing discontinuances and; 7) achieving a final relationship".

16 According to Burns and Scapens (2000, p. 16), resistance is "the reluctance to conform to new modes of thinking and behaviour, either by choice or through difficulty in adapting".

7 Conclusions

7.1 Introduction

This research examined the changes that were made to the performance measurement system (PMS) of a bank operating in an emerging economy with specific reference to the factors that influenced those changes and the consequential responses to the pressures the bank faced to change its PMS. The research addressed three research questions: (i) How did the PMS in a bank operating in Pakistan change over the last decade? (ii) What factors influenced the changes? and (iii) How did the bank respond to the factors driving change in the performance measurement system?

The research used an analytical framework developed by drawing on DiMaggio and Powell's (1983) notion of institutional isomorphism and Oliver's (1991) continuum of strategic responses to institutional pressures to address the research questions. Using the case research method, data were collected from the largest state-owned bank in Pakistan for the period 1997–2017 by administering a questionnaire and conducting semi-structured interviews. Additionally, relevant internal and external documents provided a secondary data source for the research.

As described in Chapters 5 and 6, there were significant changes in FUB's external environment, more specifically in its political, economic, technological, and socio-cultural environments. These external environmental conditions led to changes in FUB's regulatory environment (i.e., its institutional environment), and forced its managers to make changes in its PMS. These changes occurred as the result of the coercive, mimetic, and normative pressures placed on FUB. While coercive pressures were clearly present in the form of regulatory changes, the directives from the Board of Directors and the new President of the bank also provided an additional coercive pressure. Moreover, there was also evidence to suggest that the bank faced mimetic and normative pressures to change the PMS. The mimetic pressures resulted following the appointment of a new President and new business group heads, the formation of a task force and the appointment of an external consultant. In particular, the bank focused on introducing contemporary banking products and adopted innovative banking technologies by modelling other private and foreign banks. The normative pressures resulted from the increase in professionalism following the implementation of a comprehensive staff training and induction program, and from the influence of professional banking skills and knowledge applied by the new top management. FUB responded to these pressures to gain legitimacy and to promote efficiency, performance, and accountability.

The remainder of the chapter is organised as follows. Section 7.2 discusses the findings of the research in relation to each research question. Section 7.3 discusses the contributions of the research. Section 7.4 outlines the limitations of the research and provides some suggestions for further research.

7.2 The findings of the research

The analysis in this research leads to several important findings with respect to the research questions of the research.

The analysis conducted in this case research demonstrates that the change in the PMS was a direct consequence of FUB's institutional environment. This institutional environment, as shown in the book, was significantly influenced by the bank's external environment i.e., its political, economic, technological, and socio-cultural environments. The research found that FUB's external environment prior to 1997 was mainly characterised by: political instability and uncertain economic conditions. To address these conditions, the government and the regulators initiated financial sector reforms in 1997. Through these reforms, the regulators placed coercive pressures on banks to promote good governance and a culture of performance measurement and accountability. FUB responded to these pressures by changing its organisational structure and strategy and also its control systems, including its PMS. Hence, as argued in the analytical framework of this research, the research concludes that whilst macro-level factors provided indirect pressures for change in the PMS, it was the changes in the institutional environment that directly influenced FUB. The research demonstrated how FUB, being a state-owned institution, conformed to the expectations of the institutional environment and introduced various changes to gain legitimacy which was fundamental to its success.

The competitive pressures and subsequent changes in the organisational structure and strategy made FUB aware of the deficiencies in their PMS, in particular in regards to the ability of the PMS to provide required information to regulators and to support decisions in relation to its expanding business activities. This awareness stimulated the subsequent changes to FUB's PMS. The findings also demonstrate that changes in one management system can lead to change to another or other management systems. In this case structural change drove changes in the PMS. This finding further suggests that management did not just respond to the pressures to gain legitimacy but also responded to the pressures in an attempt to improve efficiency to cope with market pressures.

The research found that mimetic and normative isomorphic pressures were also influential in driving changes in the PMS. It provides evidence that these pressures were driving the bank towards securing legitimacy from its internal environment (employees, the Management Committee, and the Board of Directors) and external environment (borrowers, depositors, regulators, and government) by complying with the new regulatory requirements as well as by becoming a passive adopter of new performance measurement practices.

The research also demonstrated that while three distinct forms of institutional pressures (coercive, mimetic, and normative) were found to have affected the changes in the PMS, the nature and intensity of the institutional pressures changed over the period of analysis. For instance, all three forms of pressure played a significant role in influencing the initial changes in the PMS introduced in 2000. The subsequent changes to the PMS were mainly attributable to coercive pressures as the bank moved to comply with further regulatory changes. Later, normative pressures influenced the PMS further when the banking professionals expressed their dissatisfaction with the technological support for the PMS. This resulted in the replacement of the operating system that supported the performance measurement function within the bank.

The research also revealed that the changes that took place in the PMS were the result of a number of measures taken by the bank in response to direct coercion by the regulators. These measures included changes in the Board of Directors, the appointment of a new President, and the replacement of some senior executives. With these changes, efficiency and accountability became the new focus of the bank. Hence, the bank focused on business-like objectives, which, *inter alia*, included reductions in loan losses, diversification of products and services, and the adoption of new banking technologies. The research indicates that the pursuit of these objectives made the role of the PMS in the bank more important. Organisational members increasingly recognised the importance of measuring performance, and the PMS came to be used more in routine organisational activities as well as for planning and control purposes. More importantly, the PMS was used to provide visibility to organisational activities and to promote a sense of equity in performance measurement and accountability. Such changes in the role of the PMS appear to have contributed significantly to the development of a 'performance measurement and accountability culture' within the bank.

The above findings suggest that a bank which faces a rapidly changing organisational environment becomes increasingly keen to improve its performance, and will use the PMS more rigorously, and intensify the use of financial measures (e.g., Hussain and Hoque, 2002; Helliar et al., 2002; Cobb et al., 1995). This was clearly the case at FUB as the bank increased its performance measures from eleven in 1997 to twenty-three in 2000, and finally to forty-seven in 2003. All these performance measures were financial in nature. This finding contrasts with the previous studies on manufacturing organisations within developed countries (e.g., Tsamenyi et al., 2006; Kasurinen, 2002; Vaivio, 1999), where there is a great focus on using a combination of financial and non-financial measures to make a PMS effective. The research revealed that since FUB primarily wanted to improve financial performance by complying with the new regulatory requirements, which required extensive use of financial measures, the bank emphasised financial measures alone. Moreover, the new performance measures became part of the organisational routine as the bank commenced reviewing the bank's performance on a monthly basis in 2003 in contrast to the yearly reviews prior to 1997.

Consistent with Kaplan and Norton (1992, 1996), the research has also shown that the change in FUB's PMS was a planned and rationally executed endeavour due to its top-down initiation. The new top management, in particular the new President, took over the role of decision maker while the first-line managers (including branch managers) functioned as executors of change. The new President is referred to as a 'change agent' because he played a significant role in the change within FUB. The knowledge and experience as well as the commitment of the new President helped give the bank's new PMS its particular character. The new President was focused on improving the efficiency and performance of the bank whilst also complying with new regulatory requirements. He showed a genuine interest in changing the PMS and instigated a number of changes including setting up a task force to review FUB's management systems and appointing an external consultant to provide guidance during the PMS review. Hence, the new President played a major role in creating the performance measurement culture advocated by Radnor and Lovell (2003) and Bourne et al. (2002). In terms of DiMaggio and Powell (1983), the President also played a key role in legitimising the change in the PMS and in changing the bank's 'public sector' perception among its stakeholders.

FUB responded to the pressures to change its PMS in two ways. Initially, in the early period of the reforms, i.e., 1997, most of the impetus to change originated as formal directives from the regulators. The bank passively complied with the pressures from the regulators (i.e., coercive pressures in this case). The nature of compliance in this case was forced acquiescence (Oliver, 1991) as the bank did not have the freedom to apply strategic choice. It suggests that FUB conformed to the regulators' terms and conditions because of its dependence on them and also because of the likely financial penalties associated with non-compliance, including the potential loss of their banking licence. This finding is consistent with Oliver (1991), who suggests that when faced with coercive pressures organisations are more inclined to comply with the demands of their institutional environment rather than to avoid, defy, or manipulate it. As the performance of the banking sector gradually improved, FUB gained the freedom to exert some strategic choice while also fulfilling regulatory requirements. This was clearly observed when a change in the PMS was introduced in 2003. As the reforms proceeded, the bank increasingly applied strategic choice to the pressures, i.e., by 'balancing' with the aim not only to gain legitimacy from the regulators but also to improve efficiency and accountability. Specifically, while new performance measures were developed in line with regulatory requirements to gain legitimacy, the design of some performance measures, the branch profitability report, and the strategic planning and performance measurement process were all shaped by top management to improve efficiency and accountability.

The research found that the resistance by organisational members to the changes introduced in the PMS was minimal. This contradicts the findings of several management accounting studies (e.g., Kasurinen, 2002; Burns and Vaivio,

2001; Shields, 1995; Argyris and Kaplan, 1994). What was found in this research could be attributable to the cultural values and norms of emerging economies whereby employees are generally reluctant to complain. There was, however, an element of cynicism among employees towards the change, as to its exact nature and its likely impact on FUB staff. In particular, managers were concerned about the impact of the change on their own performance evaluation, while employees were also dissatisfied with the level of IT support provided. Poor communication of the exact nature of the PMS changes and the provision of limited training appear to be the likely causes of such dissatisfaction. The dissatisfaction with the ability of the IT system to support the new system is consistent with several management accounting studies which show that changes in PMSs are usually resisted due to the lack of infrastructure supporting the implementation of the new system (e.g., Bourne et al., 2003; Kasurinen, 2002; Cobb et al., 1995).

The research also demonstrates that the changes introduced to the PMS became institutionalised in the bank during the period under investigation. For instance, after the PMS change in 2003, the business units, in particular regional offices and branches, were able to improve reporting results to superiors. It was shown that, subsequent to the change in 2003, managers received performance measurement information on the bank's operational activities that provided the basis for follow-up, planning, and developmental activities. Further, employees used the performance measurement reports to report performance and in discussions with various business units, the Management Committee and the Board. By the time the data for this research was collected, organisational members appeared to be more accustomed to the changes and were using the new PMS extensively.

Moreover, the findings also suggest that the regional and branch managers have become more strategically focused than before. This change signifies a change in the culture of the bank from the traditional bureaucratic organisation to a commercially driven organisation. Furthermore, the analysis demonstrates that the employees were implicated in the changes to the PMS in the following ways: they have become increasingly aware of the need for performance measurement; they have noted an increase in reporting and meeting regulators' compliance requirements; and they have increased their commitment to the changed organisational environment generally, and FUB's new PMS in particular.

7.3 Contributions of the research

This research contributes to both the relevant literature and banking practices in a number of ways. These contributions are discussed in the following two subsections.

(i) Contributions to the performance measurement literature

This research contributes to three strands of literature: the performance measurement studies within the management accounting literature, the banking literature, and the literature on emerging economies. First, it provides empirical evidence on how PMSs are influenced by changes in the macro-level and institutional environments and on the way in which a bank operating in an emerging economy responded to the pressures to change its PMS. Prior studies within the performance measurement literature have failed to provide such a holistic analysis of the effect of the external environment on changes to PMSs. Further, responses to the institutional pressures influencing PMS change have generally not been addressed in the past.

Moreover, the research also makes a theoretical contribution to the management accounting literature by developing an analytical framework to examine PMS change using DiMaggio and Powell's (1983) notion of institutional isomorphism and Oliver's (1991) typology of strategic responses to institutional pressures. These theoretical constructs were used in the framework to analyse the case findings. They complement each other and allow a more plausible explanation of the changes in a PMS. By using the analytical framework, the research contributes to the literature by examining how pressures are applied from outside the organisation, explores the complex and ongoing relationship between internal organisational systems and their environment, and demonstrates how the process of PMS change is shaped by the way in which organisations respond to those pressures.

Secondly, given most previous studies have examined PMS change in the manufacturing sector, this research makes a contribution by examining PMS change in a banking context. Thirdly, by investigating changes in the PMS in an emerging economy context, the research has contributed to the existing limited evidence on the changes in performance measurement systems within emerging economies.

(ii) Contributions to performance measurement practices

The research has a number of important implications for managers of banks operating in emerging economies. First, the findings in relation to the changes experienced in FUB highlight the need for emerging economy bank managers to adapt their structure, strategy, and culture in order to be more accountable for their performance and to operate more efficiently and effectively. Managers of other emerging economy banks experiencing similar financial difficulties may learn from FUB's experience and make similar adaptations in an attempt to improve their management systems, including their PMS. While it is acknowledged that the ability of public sector banks to make such changes is dependent on government and political circumstances, it is hoped that, by highlighting the transition in the PMS of FUB, governments and bank managers in such economies will be more aware of the importance of competing on a commercial basis and keeping their PMS up to date.

Secondly, the findings highlight the importance of new regulations as the major factor influencing PMS change within FUB. Accordingly, bank managers in emerging economies need to pay close attention to regulatory changes and their impact on PMSs. The pressure to improve PMSs in banks will be far greater in the next few years following the introduction of Basel Accord III at the end of 2012. Hence, bank managers should become familiar with the anticipated impact of Basel Accord III on their PMSs, which will require banks to: maintain higher tier-1 and tier-2 risk-weighted capital ratios; use a leverage ratio as a safety net; maintain higher liquidity; use higher risk-weightings for trading assets of the bank; and exclude most of the off-balance sheet exposures from capital (Wignall and Atkinson, 2010; Lall, 2009). Banking practitioners could invest resources in monitoring and predicting potential regulatory changes, thereby enabling them to better predict and anticipate the factors likely to influence their own PMSs, and consequently allow them to prepare and adapt to such circumstances more effectively.

Thirdly, the research has identified a number of factors that could disrupt changes to an existing PMS. An understanding of such factors could assist banking practitioners to minimise disruption and also to facilitate smooth transition during the process of PMS change. For instance, the analysis highlighted that when changes in a PMS are introduced during a time when a bank is already undergoing organisational restructuring in its systems and procedures, special care must be taken to ensure that adequate time and resources are dedicated to effectively implement the new systems in order to attain required results.

Fourthly, by highlighting the successful institutionalisation of the PMS within FUB, the research indicated the vital role that change leaders play in promoting PMS change within emerging economy banks. This implies the importance of investing in suitable leaders of change for banks in emerging economies. The research also stresses the importance of providing greater autonomy to top management in public sector banks, more specifically in emerging economies, so that they are able to develop, implement, and execute strategic decisions, such as PMS change, and appoint managers who are competent and whose loyalty lies in improving the banks' performance.

Fifthly, the research demonstrates the importance for emerging economy banks of modelling best practices from industry to legitimise their operations and management systems. Similarly, emerging economy banks should invest resources in identifying best practices and continue to refine their PMSs to enhance their efficiency and effectiveness.

Finally, the research also highlighted the difference in the nature and intensity of resistance to change by organisational members when compared with existing management accounting studies conducted in developed countries. The research depicted that in emerging economies the nature of resistance to changes in the PMS was 'passive' and top management was seldom exposed to open resistance or criticism. Whatever is the nature of resistance, the research highlights that top management needs to be conscious of the factors associated with employee resistance, thereby providing banking practitioners with an improved understanding as to how to minimise resistance as they implement new PMSs. In particular, management should also ensure that they communicate the purpose and nature of new PMSs effectively to those who are directly implicated by the change and provide them with adequate training.

7.4 Limitations and directions for future research

Two limitations are identified in this research. First, the conclusions of this research are based on relevant documents and the responses to the questionnaire and interview data collected from twelve participants in one bank in an emerging economy. It is possible that issuing the questionnaire prior to the interviews has had a limiting effect on the responses provided in the interviews. Future studies may further investigate the issues addressed in this research by using different research sites and a broader range of data. Future research may also consider extending the current research by examining all three phases of changes in PMSs, namely, design, implementation, and use.

Second, the research aimed to investigate the changes in one PMS through a retrospective analysis of organisational participants' views of the change. During the interviews, participants were asked to remember issues and events which, in this case, took place up to ten years ago. There are often problems in conducting retrospective analysis since people tend to reconstruct their memories in order to make them logical or suitable for themselves or the researcher. This leads to an impending risk that valuable information from the interviewee may not reach the investigator or the researcher may not receive the information of how events actually happened. However, by having multiple data sources, the researcher was able to minimise this threat to reliability.

The limitations noted above may be addressed in future studies. It would be interesting to investigate the impact of changes in the PMS on the performance and efficiency of banks. As discussed in Chapter 1, the size, structure, strategies, and corporate culture of banks operating in the private sector within developed countries are generally different and therefore the nature and type of their performance measurement practices are also likely to be different from a state-owned bank operating in an emerging economy. Based on this view, there exists an opportunity for future studies to replicate this research in private sector banks in emerging economies.

Appendix
Interview guide

1   Can you please describe your bank's current performance measurement system?

2a   Could you please explain how many times the performance measurement system of your bank has changed during the last ten years?

2b   Can you please describe the main features of these changes?

2c   Were the changes in their performance measurement system gradual or dramatic?

3   What prompted your bank to change the performance measurement system in the past?

4   How much research did your bank do prior to initiating change in the performance measurement system?

5   What processes were used to inform and familiarise the changes in performance measurement system amongst the employees and to the business units of your bank?

6a   What was the response of employees to the change?

6b   Was there any resistance from the employees? Why?

If the reply to the question 6 b is "YES" then move to question 6c.
If the reply to the question 6 b is "No" then move to question 7a.

6c   How did you deal with their resistance?

6d   What were the features that they did not like the most?

7a   Have there been any failed attempts in changing the performance measurement system by your bank in the past?

If the reply to the question 7a is "YES" then move to question 7b.
If the reply to the question 7a is "No" then move to question 8.

7b   Could you please describe the causes of such failure?

8   Can you please describe the factors which influenced your bank the most while changing the performance measurement system?

9   How would you describe the change in your bank's business practices over the last ten years?

10   What do you perceive to be the most serious threats to your bank over the last ten years?

11a Do you think the current performance measurement system of your bank is based on an (i) organisational vision and mission (ii) corporate strategic plan?

11b Has this always been the case?

12a How frequently is performance measured in your bank at present?

12b What was the practice in the past?

13 In your opinion are business units continuously improving due to changes in the performance measurement system?

14 Do you communicate the results of the outcome of performance reviews to employees?

15 Have you linked employees' performance with their compensation plan?

16 What is your assessment of the new performance measurement system?

17 Are you aware of any shortcomings in the current performance measurement system?

18 Do you have any further comments concerning the performance measurement system within your bank which you feel is important for this research?

References

Abernethy, M. A., Bouwens, A. J. and Lent, L. (2004), 'Determinants of control system design in divisionalized firms', *The Accounting Review*, Vol. 79 No. 3, pp. 545–570.

Abernethy, M. A. and Chua, W. F. (1996), 'A field research of control systems 'redesign': the impact of institutional processes on strategic choice', *Contemporary Accounting Research*, Vol. 13 No. 2, pp. 569–606.

Abran, A. and Buglione, L. (2003), 'A multidimensional performance model for consolidating balanced scorecards', *Advanced Engineering Software*, Vol. 34 No. 6, pp. 339–349.

Ahmad, A. (1993), 'Contemporary practices of Islamic financing techniques', *IRTI Research Paper No. 20*. Jeddah: IRTI (Islamic Development Bank).

Ahmed, V. and Amjad, R. (1984), *The Management of Pakistan's Economy 1947–82*, Karachi: Oxford University Press.

Alam, M. (1997), 'Budgetary process in uncertain contexts: a research of state-owned enterprise in Bangladesh', *Management Accounting Research*, Vol. 8 No. 2, pp. 147–167.

Allen, F., McAndrews, J. and Strahan, P. (2002), 'E-finance: an introduction', *Journal of Financial Services Research*, Vol. 22 No. 12, pp. 5–27.

Almqvist, R. and Skoog, M. (2006), 'Management control transformations: change mechanisms and their constant impact on management control systems', *Journal of Human Resource Costing & Accounting*, Vol. 10 No. 3, pp. 132–154.

Amaratunga, D. and Baldry, D. (2003), 'A conceptual framework to measure facilities management performance', *Property Management*, Vol. 21 No. 2, pp. 171–189.

American Institute of Certified Public Accountants and Maisel, L. S. (2001), *Performance Measurement Practices Survey*, Jersey City, NJ: American Institute of Certified Public Accountants, Inc.

Anand, M., Sahay, B. S. and Saha, S. (2005), 'Balanced scorecard in Indian companies', *Vikalpa*, Vol. 30 No. 2, pp. 11–25.

Anderson, S. W. and Lanen, W. (1999), 'Economic transition, strategy, and the evolution of management accounting practices: the case of India', *Accounting, Organizations, and Society*, Vol. 24, pp. 379–412.

Andon, P., Baxter, J. and Chua, W. F. (2007), 'Accounting change as relational drifting: a field research of experiments with performance measurement', *Management Accounting Research*, Vol. 18, pp. 273–308.

Ang, S. and Cummings, L. L. (1997), 'Strategic responses to institutional influences on information system outsourcing', *Organizational Science*, Vol. 8 No. 3, pp. 235–256.

Anthony, R. N. (1965), *Management Planning and Control Systems: A Framework for Analysis*, Boston, MA: HBS Press.

Anthony, R. N. and Govindarajan, V. (2001), *Strategic Planning, Management Control Systems*, 10th edition, New York: McGraw-Hill/Irwin.

Anthony, R. N. and Govindarajan, V. (2007), *Management Control Systems*, 12th edition, New York: McGraw-Hill/Irwin.

Anthony, R. N., Hawkins, D. F. and Merchant, K. A. (2011), *Accounting: Text and Cases*, 13th edition, New York: McGraw-Hill/Irwin.

Argyris, C. and Kaplan, R. S. (1994), 'Implementing new knowledge: the case of activity based costing', *Accounting Horizons*, Vol. 8 No. 3, pp. 83–105.

Asian Development Bank (2002), *Guidelines for the Financial Governance and Management of Investment Projects Financed*, Manila: Asian Development Bank.

Atkinson, A. A., Balakrishnan, R., Booth, P., Cote, J. M., Groot, T., Malmi, T., Roberts, H., Uliana, E. and Wu, A. (1997), 'New directions in management accounting research', *Journal of Management Accounting Research*, Vol. 9, pp. 79–108.

Baines, A. and Langfield-Smith, K. (2003), 'Antecedents to management accounting change: a structural equation approach', *Accounting, Organizations and Society*, Vol. 28 No. 7, pp. 675–698.

Bank of England (2003), *Quarterly Bulletins*, Bank of England, London.

Bank of England (2006), *Quarterly Bulletins*, Bank of England London.

Bank of England (2008), 'The Bank's Priorities in 2008/2009', *Quarterly Bulletins*, Bank of England, London.

Bank for International Settlements (2001), Annual Report – 2001, BIS Research Department, Basel, Switzerland.

Bank for International Settlements (2003), Annual Report – 2003, BIS Research Department, Basel, Switzerland.

Bank for International Settlements (2005), Annual Report – 2005, BIS Research Department, Basel, Switzerland.

Bank for International Settlements (2006), Annual Report – 2006, BIS Research Department, Basel, Switzerland.

Bank for International Settlements (2009), Annual Reports – 2009: the global financial crisis, BIS Research Department, Basel, Switzerland.

Bank for International Settlements (2010), Annual Reports 2010, BIS Research Department, Basel, Switzerland.

Banker, R. D., Potter, G. and Schroeder, R. G. (1993), 'Reporting manufacturing performance measures to workers: an empirical investigation', *Journal of Management Accounting Research*, Vol. 3. pp. 33–55.

Banking Companies Ordinance (1947), Government of Pakistan, Islamabad.

Banking Companies Ordinance (1962), Government of Pakistan, Islamabad.

Banks Nationalisation Act (1974), Ministry of Finance, Government of Pakistan, Islamabad.

Barley, S. R. and Tolbert, P. S. (1997), 'Institutionalization and structuration: researching the links between action and institution', *Organization Studies*, Vol. 18 No. 1, pp. 93–117.

Basel Committee on Banking Supervision (2004), 'International convergence of capital measurement and capital standards – a revised framework', Bank for International Settlements, Press and Communications, CH-4002 Basel, Switzerland.

Berger, A. (2003), 'The efficiency effects of a single market for financial services in Europe', *European Journal of Operational Research*, Vol. 150, pp. 466–481.

Bernanke, B. S. (2011), 'Global imbalances: links to economic and financial stability', speech at the Banque de France Financial Stability Review Launch Event, Paris, France.

Bititci, U. S., Mendibil, K., Nudurupati, S., Turner, T. and Garengo, P. (2004), 'The interplay between performance measurement, organisational culture and management styles', *Measuring Business Excellence*, Vol. 8 No. 3, pp. 28–41.

Bititci, U. S., Nudurupati, S., Turner, T. and Creighton, S. (2002), 'Web enabled performance measurement systems', *International Journal of Operations & Production Management*, Vol. 22 No. 11, pp. 1273–1287.

Bititci, U. S., Turner, T. and Begemann, C. (2000), 'Dynamics of performance measurement systems', *International Journal of Operations and Production Management*, Vol. 20 No. 6, pp. 692–704.

Bonin, J., Hasan, I. and Wachtel, P. (2004), 'Bank performance, efficiency and ownership in transition countries', *Journal of Banking and Finance*, Vol. 29 No. 1, pp. 31–53.

Bourne, M., Mills, J., Wilcox, M., Neely, A. D. and Platts, K. (2000), 'Designing, implementing and updating performance measurement systems', *International Journal of Operations and Production Management*, Vol. 20 No. 7, pp. 754–771.

Bourne, M., Neely, A., Platts, K. and Mills, J. (2002), 'The success and failure of performance measurement initiatives: perceptions of participating managers', *International Journal of Operations and Production Management*, Vol. 22 No. 11, pp. 1288–1310.

Bourne, M., Neely, A. D., Mills, J. F. and Platts, K. W. (2003), 'Implementing performance measurement systems: a literature review', *International Journal of Business Performance Management*, Vol. 5 No. 1, pp. 1–24.

Brignall, T. J. and Modell, S. (2000), 'An institutional perspective on performance measurement and management in the new public sector', *Management Accounting Research*, Vol. 11 No. 3, pp. 281–306.

Bromwich, M. and Bhimani, A. (1989), *Management Accounting: Evolution not Revolution*, London: CIMA.

Burney, S. S. (1999), 'ANALYSIS-Small Threat Globally from Japan Megabank', *ABC NEWS Business*, August 20, 1999.

Burns, J. (2000), 'The dynamics of accounting change: inter-play between new practices, routines, institutions, power and politics', *Accounting, Auditing and Accountability Journal*, Vol. 13 No. 5, pp. 566–596.

Burns, J. and Scapens, R. W. (2000), 'Conceptualizing management accounting change: an institutional framework', *Management Accounting Research*, Vol. 11 No. 1, pp. 3–25.

Burns, J., Ezzamel, M. and Scapens, R. (1999), 'Management accounting change in the UK', *Management Accounting*, Vol. 77 No. 3, March 1999, p. 28.

Burns, J. and Vaivio, J. (2001), 'Management accounting change', *Management Accounting Research*, Vol. 12, pp. 389–402.

Carpenter, V. L. and Feroz, E. H. (1992), 'GAAP as a symbol of legitimacy: New York state's decision to adopt generally accepted accounting principles', *Accounting, Organization and Society*, Vol. 17 No. 7, pp. 613–643.

Carruthers, B. (1995), 'Accounting, ambiguity, and the new institutionalism', *Accounting, Organizations, and Society*, Vol. 20, pp. 313–328.

Chan, Y.-C. L. (2004), 'Performance measurement and adoption of balanced scorecards: a survey of municipal governments in the USA and Canada', *The International Journal of Public Sector Management*, Vol. 17 No. 3, pp. 204–221.

Chapman, C. S. (1997), 'Reflections on a contingent view of accounting', *Accounting, Organizations and Society*, Vol. 22, pp. 189–205.

Chenhall, R. H. (2003), 'Management control systems design within its organizational context: findings from contingency-based research and directions for future', *Accounting, Organizations and Society*, Vol. 28 No. 2–3, pp. 127–168.

Chenhall, R. H. (2005), 'Integrative strategic performance measurement systems, strategic alignment of manufacturing, learning and strategic outcomes: an exploratory research', *Accounting, Organizations and Society*, Vol. 30, pp. 395–422.

Chenhall, R. H. and Euske, K. J. (2007), 'The role of management control systems in planned organizational change: an analysis of two organizations', *Accounting, Organizations and Society*, Vol. 32, pp. 601–637.

Chenhall, R. H. and Morris, D. (1995), 'Organic decision and communication processes and management accounting systems in entrepreneurial and conservative business organizations', *Omega*, Vol. 23 No. 5, pp. 485–497.

Chia, Y. (1995), 'Decentralization, management accounting (MCS) information characteristics and their interaction effects on managerial performance: a Singapore research', *Journal of Business Finance and Accounting*, Vol. 22 No. 6, pp. 811–830.

Chow, C. W., Haddad, K. M. and Williamson, J. E. (1997), 'Applying the balanced scorecard to small companies', *Management Accounting*, Vol. LXXIX No. 2, pp. 21–27.

Chow, C. W., Shields, M. D. and Wu, A. (1999), 'The importance of national culture in the design of and preference for management control for multinational operations', *Accounting, Organisations and Society*, Vol. 24 No. 5/6, pp. 441–461.

Chow, C. W. and Van der Stede, W. A. (2006), 'The use and usefulness of non-financial performance measures', *Management Accounting*, Vol. 7 No. 3, pp. 1–8.

CIMA (1993), *Performance measurement in the manufacturing sector*, London: Chartered Institute of Management Accountants.

Citigroup Inc. (2000), Annual Report – 2000, (www. CITIGROUP.com), Brooklyn, NY.

Claessens, S. and Laeven, L. (2003), '*What drives bank competition? Some international evidence*', Policy Research Working Paper no: WPS3113, The World Bank Financial Sector Operations and Policy Department, Washington, DC: World Bank.

Cobb, I., Helliar, C. and Innes, J. (1995), 'Management accounting change in a bank', *Management Accounting Research*, Vol. 6 No. 2, pp. 155–176.

Covaleski, M. A. and Dirsmith, M. W. (1988), 'The use of budgetary symbols in the political arena: an historically informed field research', *Accounting, Organizations and Society*, Vol. 13 No. 1, pp. 1–24.

Covaleski, M. A., Dirsmith, M. W. and Michelman, J. E. (1993), 'An institutional theory perspective on the DRG framework case-mix accounting systems and health-care organizations', *Accounting, Organizations and Society*, Vol. 18 No. 1, pp. 65–80.

Creswell, J. W. (1994), *Research Design: Qualitative & Quantitative Approaches*, Thousand Oaks, CA: Sage.

Cull, R. and Peria, M. (2007), '*Foreign Banks Participations and Crises in Developing Countries*', World Bank Policy Research Working Paper 4128, Washington, DC.

Damanpour, F. and Evan, W. M. (1984), 'Organizational innovation and performance: the problem of organizational lag', *Administrative Science Quarterly*, Vol. 29, pp. 392–409.

Das, H. (1983), 'Qualitative research in organizational behaviour', *Journal of Management Studies*, Vol. 20, pp. 1–34.

Dent, E. B. and Goldberg, S. G. (1999), 'Challenging "resistance to change"', *Journal of Applied Behavioural Sciences*, Vol. 35 No. 11, pp. 25–41.

Dent, J. (1990), 'Strategy, organisation and control: some possibilities for accounting research', *Accounting, Organisations and Society*, Vol. 15 No. 1/2, pp. 3–25.

De Waal, A. A. (2007), 'Is performance management applicable in developing countries? The case of a Tanzanian college', *International Journal of Emerging Markets*, Vol. 2 No. 1, pp. 69–83.

Dillard, J. M. and Reilly, R. R. (1988), *Systematic Interviewing: Communication Skills for Professional Effectiveness*, Columbus, OH: Merrill.

Dillman, D. A. (1999), 'Mail and other self administered surveys in the 21st Century: the beginning of a new era', *The Gallup Research Journal*, Winter/Spring, pp. 121–140.

DiMaggio, P. J. and Powell, W. W. (1983), 'The iron cage revisited: institutional isomorphism and collective rationality in organizational fields', *American Sociological Review*, Vol. 48 No. 2, pp. 147–160.

DiMaggio, P. J. and Powell, W. W. (1991), 'Introduction', in Powell, W. W. and DiMaggio, P. J. (Eds.), *The New Institutionalism in Organizational Analysis*, Chicago: The University of Chicago Press, pp. 1–38.

Dixon, J. R., Nanni, A. J. and Vollmann, T. E. (1990), *The New Performance Challenge – Measuring Operations for World-Class Competition*, Homewood, IL: Business One Irwin.

Dowling, J. and Pfeffer, J. (1975), 'Organisational legitimacy: social values and organisational behaviour', *Pacific Sociological Review*, Vol. 18 No. 1, pp. 122–136.

Downing, L. M. (2001), '*The Global BSC Community: A Special Report on Implementation Experience from Scorecard Users Worldwide*', Paper presented at the Balanced Scorecard European Summit, Nice.

Drucker, P. F. (2003), *The New Realities*, New York: Transaction Publishers.

Drury, C. (2002), *Management and Cost Accounting*, 5th edition, London: Thomson.

Drury, C., Braund, S., Osborne, P. and Tayles, M. (1993), *A Survey of Management Accounting Practices in UK Manufacturing Companies*, London: Chartered Association of Certified Accountants.

Drury, C. and Tyles, M. (1995), 'Issues arising from surveys of management accounting practices', *Management Accounting Research*, Vol. 6 No. 3, pp. 267–280.

Dunk, A. S. (1992), 'Reliance on budgetary control, manufacturing process automation and production sub-unit performance: a research note', *Accounting, Organizations and Society*, Vol. 17 No. 3–4, pp. 195–203.

Eccles, R. G. (1991), 'The performance measurement manifesto', *Harvard Business Review*, January–February, pp. 131–137.

Eccles, R. G. (1998), 'The performance measurement manifesto', in *Measuring Corporate Performance*, Boston, MA: Harvard Business Review, pp. 25–45.

Economic Survey of Pakistan (1996), *Ministry of Finance*, Islamabad: Government of Pakistan.

Economic Survey of Pakistan (1997), *Ministry of Finance*, Islamabad: Government of Pakistan.

Economic Survey of Pakistan (2010), *Ministry of Finance*, Islamabad: Government of Pakistan.

Edwards, J. and Ogilvie, S. (1996), 'Universal banks and German industrialization: a reappraisal', *Economic History Review*, pp. 427–446.

Efferin, S. and Hopper, T. (2007), 'Management control, culture and ethnicity in a Chinese Indonesian company', *Accounting, Organizations and Society*, Vol. 32, pp. 223–262.

Eisenhardt, K. M. (1989), 'Building theories from case research', *Academy of Management Review*, Vol. 14 No. 4, pp. 532–550.

Emmanuel, C., Otley, D. and Merchant, K. A. (1990), *Accounting for Management Control*, 2nd edition, London: Chapman and Hall.

Errico, L. and Farahbaksh, M. (1998), '*Islamic banking: Issues in prudential regulations and supervision*', Working Paper WP/98/30, International Monetary Fund, Washington DC.

Farrell, T. (1996), 'Figuring out fighting organisations: the new organisational analysis in strategic studies', *Journal of Strategic Studies*, Vol. 19 No. 1, pp. 122–135.

Ferreira, A. and Otley, D. (2009), 'The design and use of performance management systems: an extended framework for analysis', *Management Accounting Research*, Vol. 20, pp. 263–282.

Firth, M. (1996), 'The diffusion of managerial accounting procedures in the People's Republic of China and the influence of foreign partnered joint ventures', *Accounting, Organizations and Society*, Vol. 21 No. 7/8, pp. 629–654.

Fitzgerald, L., Johnston, R., Brignall, T. J., Silvestro, R. and Voss, C. (1991), *Performance measurement in service businesses*, London: Chartered Institute of Management Accountants, London.

Flamholtz, E. G. (1983), 'Accounting, budgeting and control systems in their organizational context: theoretical and empirical perspectives', *Accounting, Organizations and Society*, Vol. 8 No. 2/3, pp. 153–169.

Fligstein, N. (1985), 'The spread of the multidivisional form among large firms, 1919–1979', *American Sociological Review*, Vol. 50 No. 3, pp. 377–391.

Fossey, E., Harvey, C., McDermott, F. and Davidson, L. (2002), 'Understanding and evaluating qualitative research', *Australia New Zealand Journal of Psychiatry*, Vol. 36 No. 6, pp. 717–732.

Francis, H. (2002), 'A bias for talk, HRM and the reconstruction of employee relations', *Personnel Review*, Vol. 31 No. 4, pp. 432–448.

Frank, K. A. and Fahrbach, K. (1999), 'Organization culture as a complex system: balance and information in models of influence and selection', *Organization Science*, Vol. 10 No. 3, pp. 253–277.

Frei, F. X., Harker, P. T. and Hunter, L. W. (1998), '*Innovation in retail banking*', Working paper, Financial Institutions Center, The Wharton School, University of Pennsylvania, Philadelphia, PA, pp. 1–44.

Fries, S. and Taci, A. (2005), '*Banking reform and development in transition economies*', European Bank for Reconstruction and Development Working Paper 71, London, UK.

Fries, S., Neven, D. and Seabright, P. (2002), '*Bank performance in transition economies*', European Bank for Reconstruction and Development Working Paper, No. 76, London, UK.

Frigo, M. L. and Krumwiede, K. R. (1999), 'Balanced scorecards: a rising trend in strategic performance measurement', *Journal of Strategic Performance Measurement*, Vol. 3 No. 1, pp. 42–44.

FUB (1995), Annual Report – 1995, Karachi, Pakistan.

FUB (1996), Annual Report – 1996, Karachi, Pakistan.

FUB (1997), Annual Report – 1997, Karachi, Pakistan.

FUB (1999), Annual Report – 1999, Karachi, Pakistan.

FUB (2000), Annual Report – 2000, Karachi, Pakistan.

FUB (2001), Annual Report – 2001, Karachi, Pakistan.

FUB (2004), FUB Compliance Review Manual, Karachi, Pakistan.

FUB (2005), Annual Report – 2005, Karachi, Pakistan.

Fuller, T. (1999), 'Midsized operations hit hard by shakeout: Asian banks count cost', published in *International Herald Tribune*, Wednesday, May 19, 1999.

Garengo, P., Nudurupati, S. and Bititci, U. S. (2007), 'Understanding the relationship between PMS and MIS in SMEs: the key role of organizational development', *Computers in Industry*, Vol. 58 No. 7, pp. 677–686.

Geyfman, V. (2005), '*Risk-adjusted performance measures at bank holding companies with section 20 subsidiaries*', Working paper no. 05–26, Research Department, Federal Reserve Bank of Philadelphia, PA.

Ghalayini, A. M. and Noble, J. S. (1996), 'The changing basis of performance measurement', *International Journal of Operations & Production Management*, Vol. 16 No. 8, pp. 63–80.

Ghalayini, A. M., Noble, J. S. and Crowe, T. J. (1997), 'An integrated dynamic performance measurement system for improving manufacturing competitiveness', *International Journal of Production Economics*, Vol. 48 No. 3, pp. 207–225.

Gormley, T. A. (2007), 'Banking competition in developing countries: does foreign bank entry improve credit access?', The Wharton School, University of Pennsylvania, Philadelphia.

Granlund, M. and Lukka, K. (1998), 'It's a small world of management accounting practices', *Journal of Management Accounting Research*, Vol. 10, pp. 153–179.

Greenwood, R. and Hinings, C. R. (1996), 'Understanding radical organizational change: bringing together the old and the new institutionalism', *Academy of Management Review*, Vol. 21 No. 4, pp. 1022–1054.

Greve, H. R. (2000), 'Market niche entry decisions: competition, learning, and strategy in Tokyo banking, 1894–1936', *The Academy of Management Journal*, Vol. 43 No. 4, pp. 816–836.

Guba, E. G. and Lincoln, Y. S. (1994), 'Competing paradigms in qualitative research', in Denzin and Lincoln (Eds), *Handbook of Qualitative Research*, Thousand Oaks, CA: SAGE.

Guerreiro, R., Alberto, C. and Frezatti, F. (2006), 'Evaluating management accounting change according to the institutional theory approach: a case research of a Brazilian bank' *Journal of Accounting & Organizational Change*, Vol. 2 No. 3, pp. 196–228.

Hannan, A. (2005), 'Innovating in higher education: contexts for change in learning technology', *British Journal of Educational Technology*, Vol. 36 No. 6, pp. 975–985.

Haque, N. U. and Kardar, S. (1995), 'The development of financial markets in Pakistan', Asian Development Bank Asian Development Bank, Manila.

Harker, P. T. and Zenios, S. A. (1998), '*What drives the performance of financial institutions?*', Working paper, Financial Institutions Center, The Wharton School, University of Pennsylvania, Philadelphia, PA, pp. 1–27.

Hartmann, F. G. H. (2000), 'The appropriateness of RAPM: towards the further development of theory', *Accounting, Organizations and Society*, Vol. 25, pp. 451–482.

Hawkins, J. and Mihaljek, D. (2001), 'The banking industry in the emerging market economies: competition, consolidation and systematic stability – An overview', Monetary and Economic Department, Bank of International Settlements, Basel, Switzerland, pp. 1–44.

Helliar, C., Cobb, I. and Innes, J. (2002), 'A longitudinal case research of profitability reporting in a bank', *British Accounting Review*, Vol. 34, pp. 27–53.

Hilbers, P., Krueger, R. and Moretti, M. (2000), 'New tools for assessing financial system soundness', *Finance and Development, International Monetary Fund*, Vol. 37 No. 3, pp. 8–12.

Hitt, L. and Frei, F. (2002), 'Do better customers utilize electronic distribution channels? The case of PC banking', *Management Science*, Vol. 48 No. 6, pp. 732–749.

Hoffman, A. J. (1999), 'Institutional evolution and change: environmentalism and the U.S. chemical industry', *Academy of Management Journal*, Vol. 42, pp. 451–471.

Hofstede, G. H. (1984), 'Cultural dimensions in management and planning', *Asia Pacific Journal of Management*, Vol. 1 No. 2, pp. 81–99.

Holland, C. P., Lockett, A. G. and Blackman, I. D. (1997), 'The impact of globalisation and information technology on the strategy and profitability of the banking industry', *System Sciences*, Vol. 3, pp. 418–427.

Homburg, C., Workman, J. P. and Krohmer, H. (1999), 'Marketing's influence within the firm', *Journal of Marketing*, Vol. 63, pp. 1–17.

Hopper, T. and Powell, A. (1985), 'Making sense of research into the organizational and social aspects of management accounting: a review of its underlying assumptions', *Journal of Management Studies*, Vol. 22 No. 5, pp. 429–465.

Hoque, Z. and Alam, M. (1999), 'TQM adoption institutionalization and changes in management accounting systems: a case research', *Accounting and Business Research*, Vol. 29, pp. 199–210.

Hoque, Z. and Hopper, T. (1994), 'Rationality, accountability and politics: a case research of management control in Bangladeshi Jute Mill', *Management Accounting Research*, Vol. 5, pp. 5–30.

Hoque, Z. and Hopper, T. (1997), 'Political and industrial relations: turbulence, competition and budgeting in the nationalized jute mills of Bangladesh', *Accounting and Business Research*, Vol. 27 No. 2, pp. 125–143.

Hoque, Z. and James, W. (2000), 'Linking balanced scorecard measures with size and market factors: impact on organisational performance', *Journal of Management Accounting Research*, Vol. 12, pp. 1–17.

Hussain, M. M. (2003), 'The impact of economic conditions on management accounting performance measures: experience with banks', *Managerial Finance*, Vol. 29 No. 2/3, pp. 23–41.

Hussain, M. M. and Gunasekaran, A. (2002), 'An institutional perspective of non-financial accounting measures: a review of the financial services industry', *Managerial Auditing Journal*, Vol. 17, pp. 518–536.

Hussain, M. M. and Hoque, Z. (2002), 'Understanding non-financial performance measurement practices in Japanese banks: a new institutional sociology perspective', *Accounting, Auditing and Accountability Journal*, Vol. 15 No. 2, pp. 162–183.

Iimi, A. (2004), 'Banking sector reforms in Pakistan: economies of scale and scope, and cost complementarities', *Journal of Asian Economics*, Vol. 15, pp. 507–528.

Innes, J. and Mitchell, F. (1990), 'The process of change in management accounting: some field research evidence', *Management Accounting Research*, Vol. 1 No. 1, pp. 3–19.

Ittner, C. D. and Larcker, D. F. (1998), 'Innovations in performance measurement: trends and research implications', *Journal of Management Accounting Research*, Vol. 10, pp. 205–238.

Jepperson, R. L. (1991), '*Institutions, institutional effects and institutionalism*', in the new institutionalism in organizational analysis by Powell, W. W. and DiMaggio, P. J. (Eds), Chicago: The University of Chicago press, pp. 143–163.

Jeucken, M. H. A. and Bouma, J. J. (1999), 'The changing environment of banks', GMI Theme Issue: Sustainable Banking: The Greening of Finance, Netherlands, pp. 21–35. Accessed on 20/06/2018 https://sustfin.eu/assets/Articles-news/1023882966/1999-gmi-jeucken-bouma.pdf

Johnson, H. T. and Kaplan, R. S. (1987), *Relevance Lost – The Rise and Fall of Management Accounting*, Boston, MA: Harvard Business School Press.

Jones, C. S. (1985), 'An empirical research of the role of management accounting systems following takeover or merger', *Accounting, Organizations and Society*, pp. 177–200.

Kahveci, E. and Sayılgan, G. (2006), 'Globalization of financial markets and its effects on central banks and monetary policy strategies: Canada, New Zealand and UK Case with inflation targeting', *International Research Journal of Finance and Economics*, Vol. 1, pp. 86–101.

Kanji, G. K. and Moura, P. E. (2002), 'Kanji's business scorecard – Quality assurance and total quality management', *Total Quality Management and Business Excellence*, Vol. 13 No. 1, pp. 13–27.

Kaplan, R. S. (1984), 'The evaluation of management accounting', *The Accounting Review*, Vol. 56 No. 3, pp. 390–418.

Kaplan, R. S. and Norton, D. P. (1992), 'The balanced scorecard – Measures that drive performance', *Harvard Business Review*, Vol. 70 No. 1, pp. 71–79.

Kaplan, R. S. and Norton, D. P. (1996), *The Balanced Scorecard – Translating Strategy into Action*, Boston, MA: Harvard Business School Press.

Kaplan, R. S. and Norton, D. P. (2001), *The Strategy-Focused Organization: How Balanced Scorecard Companies Thrive in the New Business Environment*, Boston, MA: Harvard Business School Press.

Karr, J. (1997), 'Line-of-business performance: 1995 disclosures and best practices', *The Journal of Bank Accounting and Finance*, Winter: 1997, pp. 36–42.

Kasurinen, T. (2002), 'Exploring management accounting change: the case of balanced scorecard implementation', *Management Accounting Research*, Vol. 13, pp. 323–343.

Kaufman, G. G., Krueger, T. H. and Hunter, W. C. (1999), *The Asian Financial Crisis: Origins, Implications and Solutions*, London: Springer.

Keegan, D. P., Eiler, R. G. and Jones, C. R. (1989), 'Are your performance measures obsolete?', *Management Accounting*, Vol. 71, pp. 45–50.

Kennerley, M. P. and Neely, A. D. (2002), 'A framework of the factors affecting the evolution of performance measurement systems', *International Journal of Operations & Production Management*, Vol. 22 No. 11, pp. 1222–1245.

Kennerley, M. P. and Neely, A. D. (2003), 'Measuring performance in a changing business environment', *International Journal of Operations and Production Management*, Vol. 23 No. 2, pp. 213–229.

Khan, A. A. (2005), *Economics*, 1st edition, Karachi: Institute of Bankers Pakistan.

Khan, M. A., Farooq, A. and Amin, L. (2000), 'Disaggregated approach for modeling demand for money in Pakistan', *Pakistan Journal of Applied Economics*, vol. 16, pages 65–77.

Khandwalla, P. N. (1972), 'The effect of different types of competition on the use of management controls', *Journal of Accounting Research*, Autumn 1972, pp. 275–285.

Khandwalla, P. N. (1977), *Design of Organisations*, New York: Harcourt Brace Jonanovich.

Kimball, R. C. (1997), 'Innovations in performance measurement in banking', *New England Economic Review*, May/June, pp. 23–38.

Kirk, J. and Miller, M. L. (1986), *Reliability and Validity in Qualitative Research*, Beverly Hills: Sage.

Kotter, J. P. and Schlesinger, L. A. (1979), 'Choosing strategies for change', *Harvard Business Review*, Vol. 57, pp. 106–114.

Krumwiede, K. R. and Charles, S. L. (2006), 'Finding the right mix: how to match strategy and management practices to enhance firm performance', *Strategic Finance*, Vol. 87 No. 10, pp. 37–43.

Lall, R. (2009), '*Why Basel II failed and why any Basel III is doomed*', GEG working paper, 2009/52, Department of Politics and International Relations, University College, Oxford UK, pp. 1–31.

Langfield-Smith, K. (1997), 'Management control systems and strategy: a critical review', *Accounting, Organizations and Society*, Vol. 22 No. 2, pp. 207–232.

Langfield-Smith, K., Thorne, H. and Hilton, R. W. (2009), *Management Accounting: information for Managing and Creating Value*, 5th edition, Melbourne Australia: McGraw-Hill.

Lapavitsas, C. and Santos, P. L. D. (2008), 'Globalisation and contemporary banking: on the impact of new technology', *Contributions to Political Economy*, Vol. 27, pp. 31–56.

Libby, T. and Waterhouse, J. H. (1996), 'Predicting change in management accounting systems', *Journal of Management Accounting Research*, Vol. 8, pp. 137–150.

Lord, B. R. (2007), 'Strategic management accounting', in Hopper, T., Northcott, D. and Scapens, R. (Eds), *Issues in Management Accounting*, 3rd edition, Harlow: FT Prentice Hall, pp. 135–153.

Lowe, T. and Puxty, T. (1989), 'The problems of a paradigm: a critique of the prevailing orthodoxy in management control', in Wai Fong Chua, Lowe, T. and Puxty, T. (Eds), *Critical Perspectives in Management Control*, Palgrave Macmillan Press London UK, pp. 9–26.

Lynch, R. L. and Cross, K. F. (1991), *Measure Up – The Essential Guide to Measuring Business Performance*, London: Mandarin – Blackwell.

Marginson, S. and Considine, M. (2000), *The Enterprise University: Power, Governance and Reinvention in Australia*, Cambridge/London: Cambridge University Press.

Marshall, M., Lyle, W., Paul, E. and Stuart, G. (1999), '21st century focus: better results by linking citizens, government, and performance measurement', *Public Management*, November 1999, pp. 12–18.

Maskell, B. (1989), 'Performance measurement for world class manufacturing', *Management Accounting*, Vol. May, pp. 32–33.

McAdam, R., Hazlett, S. A. and Casey, C. (2005), 'Performance management in the UK public sector: addressing multiple stakeholder complexity', *The International Journal of Public Sector Management*, Vol. 18 No. 3, pp. 256–273.

McColl-Kennedy, J. R. and Anderson, R. D. (2005), 'Subordinate-manager gender combination and perceived leadership style influence on emotions, self-esteem and organizational commitment', *Journal of Business Research*, Vol. 58 No. 2, pp. 115–125.

McCunn, P. (1998), 'The balanced scorecard: the eleventh commandment', *Management Accounting – London*, Vol. 76 No. 11, pp. 34–36.

McKendrick, D. (1995), 'Sources of imitation: improving bank process capabilities', *Research Policy*, Vol. 24, pp. 783–802.

McKinnon, J. (1988), 'Reliability and validity in field research: some strategies and tactics', *Accounting, Auditing and Accountability*, Vol. 1 No. 1, pp. 34–54.

Meenai, S. A. (2001), *Money and Banking in Pakistan*, Revised and Expanded Edition by Javed A. Ansari, Karachi: Oxford University Press.

Melnyk, S. A., Stewart, D. M. and Swink, M. (2004), 'Metrics and performance measurement in operations management: dealing with the metrics maze', *Journal of Operations Management*, Vol. 22, pp. 209–217.

Merchant, K. A. (1984), 'Influences on departmental budgeting: an empirical examination of a contingency model', *Accounting Organizations and Society*, Vol. 9 No. (3/4), pp. 291–307.

Merchant, K. A. (1990), 'The effects of financial controls on data manipulation and management myopia', *Accounting, Organizations and Society*, Vol. 15, pp. 297–313.

Merchant, K. A. (1998), *Modern Management Control Systems: Text and Cases*, New Jersey: Prentice-Hall.

Merchant, K. A. and Van der Stede, W. (2007), *Management Control Systems: Performance Measurement, Evaluation and Incentives*, 2nd edition, California: Financial Times Press – Prentice Hall.

Meyer, J. W. and Rowan, B. (1977), 'Institutionalized organizations: formal structure as myth and ceremony', *American Journal of Sociology*, Vol. 83, pp. 340–363.

Meyer, J. W. and Rowan, B. (1991), 'Institutionalised organizations: formal structure as myth and ceremony', in Powell, W. and DiMaggio, P. (Eds), *The New Institutionalism in Economic Analysis*, Chicago, IL: University of Chicago Press, pp. 41–63.

Meyer, M. W. (2002), *Rethinking Performance Measurement: Beyond the Balanced Scorecard*, Cambridge: Cambridge University Press.

Miles, R. E. and Snow, C. C. (1978), *Organizational Strategy, Structure and Process*, New York: McGraw-Hill.

Modell, S. (2007), 'Managing accounting change', in *Issues in Management Accounting*, Hopper, T., Northcott, D. and Scapens, R. (Eds), 3rd edition, Harlow: FT Prentice Hall, pp. 335–355.

Moreno, R. (2003), 'Fiscal issues and central banking in emerging economies: an overview', BIS papers, in *Bank for International Settlements*, Vol. 20, pp. 1–9.

Murray, T. R. (2003), *Blending Qualitative and Quantitative Research Methods in Theses and Dissertations*, Thousand Oaks, CA: Corwin Press.

Neely, A. D. (1998), *Measuring Business Performance – Why, What and How*, London: Economist Books.

Neely, A. D. (1999), 'The performance measurement revolution: why now and what next?', *International Journal of Operations and Production Management*, Vol. 19 No. 2, pp. 205–228.

Neely, A. D. and Adams, C. (2001), 'The performance prism perspective', *Journal of Cost Management*, Vol. 5 No. 1, pp. 7–15.

Neely, A. D., Adams, C. and Crowe, P. (2001), 'The performance prism in practice – Measuring business excellence', *Journal of Cost Management*, Vol. 5 No. 2, pp. 6–11.

Neely, A. D., Adams, C. and Kennerley, M. P. (2002), *The Performance Prism: The Scorecard for Measuring and Managing Business Success*, London: Financial Times-Prentice Hall.

Neely, A. D., Gregory, M. and Platts, K. (1995), 'Performance measurement system design: a literature review and research agenda', *International Journal of Operations & Production Management*, Vol. 15 No. 4, pp. 80–116.

Neely, A. D., Mills, J., Platts, K., Gregory, M. and Richards, H. (1994), 'Realising strategy through measurement', *International Journal of Operations and Production Management*, Vol. 14 No. 3, pp. 140–152.

Neuman, L. W. (2004), *Social Research Methods: Qualitative and Quantitative Approaches*, 6th edition, Boston, MA: Allyn and Bacon.

Norreklit, H. (2000), 'The balance on the balanced scorecard – A critical analysis of some of its assumptions', *Management Accounting Research*, Vol. 11, pp. 65–88.

O'Connor, N. G. (1995), 'The influence of organizational culture in the usefulness of budget participation by Singaporean-Chinese managers', *Accounting, Organizations, and Society*, Vol. 20 No. 5, pp. 383–403.

O'Connor, N. G., Chow, C. W. and Wu, A. (2004), 'The adoption of "Western" management accounting/controls in China's state-owned enterprises during economic transition', *Accounting, Organizations and Society*, Vol. 29 No. 3/4, pp. 349–375.

Oliver, C. (1991), 'Strategic responses to institutional processes', *Academy of Management Review*, Vol. 16 No. 1, pp. 145–179.

Olson, E. M. and Slater, S. F., (2002), 'The balanced scorecard, competitive strategy and performance', *Business Horizons*, Vol. 45 No. 3, pp. 11–16.

O'Neill, H. M., Pouder, R. W. and Buchholtz, A. H. (1998), 'Pattern in the diffusion of strategies across organizations: insights from the innovation diffusion literature', *Academy of Management Review*, Vol. 23 No. 1, pp. 98–114.

Otley, D. (1994), 'Management control in contemporary organizations: towards a wider framework', *Management Accounting Research*, Vol. 5 No. 3, pp. 289–299.

Otley, D. (1999), 'Performance management: a framework for management control systems research', *Management Accounting Research*, Vol. 10 No. 10, pp. 363–382.

Otley, D. and Berry, A. J. (1994), 'Case research in accounting and control', *Management Accounting Research*, Vol. 5, pp. 45–65.

Otley, D., Broadbent, J. and Berry, A. (1995), 'Research in management control: an overview of its development', *British Journal of Management*, Vol. 6 (special issue), pp. 31–44.

Patton, M. Q. (2001), *Qualitative Evaluation Methods*, Newbury Park, CA: Sage.

Patton, M. Q. (2002), *Qualitative Research and Evaluation Methods*, Thousand Oaks, CA: Sage.

Perera, S. (2004), 'The impact of contextual changes on management accounting practices: evidence from a government trading enterprise in Australia', *International Journal of Accounting, Auditing and Performance Evaluation*, Vol. 1 No. 4, pp. 465–492.

Perera, S., McKinnon, J. and Harrison, G. (2003), 'Diffusion of transfer pricing innovation in a public sector organization: a longitudinal case research', *Management Accounting Research*, Vol. 14 No. 2, pp. 140–164.

Perera, S., Schoch, H. and Sabaratnam, S. (2007), 'Adoption of the balanced scorecard in a non-profit setting: evidence from local government', *Asia-Pacific Management Accounting Journal*, Vol. 2 No. 1, pp. 53–70.

Pettigrew, A. M. (1979), 'On researching organisational cultures', *Administrative Science Quarterly*, Vol. 24, pp. 570–581.

Pfeffer, J. and Salancik, G. R. (1978), *The External Control of Organizations: A Resource Dependence Perspective*, New York: Harper & Row.

PriceWaterhouseCoopers (2009), *The Future of Banking: Returning Stability to the Banks and the Banking System*, UK: PricewaterhouseCoopers International Limited.

PriceWaterhouseCoopers (2011), *Organisational Transformation: What is Internal Audit's Role?* Australia: PricewaterhouseCoopers International Limited.

Pun, K. F. and White, A. S. (2005), 'A performance measurement paradigm for integrating strategy formulation: a review of systems and frameworks', *International Journal of Management Reviews*, Vol. 7 No. 1, pp. 49–71.

Radnor, Z. J. and Lovell, B. (2003), 'Success factors for implementation of the balanced scorecard in a NHS multi-agency setting', *International Journal of Health Care Quality Assurance*, Vol. 16 No. 2, pp. 99–108.

Reid, G. C. and Smith, J. A. (1999), 'Information system development in the small firm: tests of contingency, agency and markets and hierarchies approach', (http://ww.ideas.repec.org/p/san/crieff/9905.html).

Reserve Bank of Australia (2010), *Economic Outlook, Statement on Monetary Policy*, Sydney: Reserve Bank of Australia.

Rigby, D. (2001), 'Management tools and techniques: a survey', *California Management Review*, Vol. 43 No. 2, pp. 139–160.

Rogers, E. M. (1995), *Diffusion of Innovation*, 4th edition, New York: Free Press.

Rogers, E. M. and Shoemaker, F. F. (1971), *Communication of Innovation: A Cross Cultural-Approach*, New York: Free Press.

Ryan, B., Scapens, R. W. and Theobold, M. (2002), *Research Method and Methodology in Finance and Accounting*, 2nd edition, London: Thompson.

Sarbanes Oxley Act (2002), Washington, DC, (http://fl1.findlaw.com/news.findlaw.com/hdocs/docs/gwbush/sarbanesoxley072302.pdf).

Sartorius, K., Eitzen, C. and Nicholson, C. (2006), 'The appropriateness of performance measurement in the services sector: a case research', *South African Journal of Accounting Research*, Vol. 20 No. 1, pp. 27–50.

Scapens, R. W. (1994), 'Never mind the gap: towards an institutional perspective on management accounting practice', *Management Accounting Research*, Vol. 5 No. 3/4, pp. 301–321.

Scapens, R. W. (2006), 'Understanding management accounting practices: a personal journey', *The British Accounting Review*, Vol. 38, pp. 1–30.

Scapens, R. W. and Roberts, J. (1993), 'Accounting control: a case research of resistance to accounting change', *Management Accounting Research*, Vol. 4 No. 1, pp. 1–32.

Scott, W. R. (1987), 'The adolescence of institutional theory', *Administrative Science Quarterly*, Vol. 32 No. 4, pp. 493–511.

Scott, W. R. (1992), *Organizations: Rational, Natural, and Open Systems*, 3rd edition, Englewood Cliffs, NJ: Prentice Hall.

Scott, W. R. (1995), *Institutions and Organizations*, Thousand Oaks, CA: Sage.

Scott, W. R. (1998), *Organisations: Rational, Natural and Open System*, London: Prentice-hall.

Scott, W. R. (2001), *Institutions and Organisations*, 2nd edition, Thousand Oaks, CA: Sage.

Shields, M. D. (1995), 'An empirical analysis of firms: implementation experiences with activity-based costing', *Journal of Management Accounting Research*, pp. 148–166.

Shields, M. D. and Young, S. M. (1989), 'A behavioral model for implementing cost management systems', *Journal of Cost Management*, pp. 17–27.

Silk, S. (1998), 'Automating the balanced scorecard', *Management Accounting*, Vol. 11 No. 17, pp. 38–44.

Simons, R. (1990), 'The role of management control systems in creating competitive advantage: new perspectives', *Accounting, Organizations and Society*, Vol. 15 No. 1–2, pp. 127–143.

Sinclair, D. and Zairi, M. (2000), 'Performance measurement: a critical analysis of the literature with respect to total quality management', *International Journal of Management Review*, Vol. 2 No. 2, pp. 145–168.

Siti-Nabiha, A. K. and Scapens, R. W. (2005), 'Stability and change: an institutionalist research of management accounting change', *Accounting Auditing and Accountability Journal*, Vol. 18, pp. 44–73.

Soin, K. (1996), '*Organisational change and the introduction of activity based costing in a UK clearing bank*', working paper, Sheffield Hallam University, Sheffield UK.

Soin, K., Seal, W. and Cullen, J. (2002), 'ABC and organizational change: an institutional perspective', *Management Accounting Research*, Vol. 13, pp. 249–271.

Stark, D. (1996), 'Recombinant property in East European Capitalism', *American Journal of Sociology*, Vol. 101 No. 4, pp. 993–1027.

State Bank of Pakistan (1990), Annual Report – 1990, (www.sbp.org.pk), Karachi.

State Bank of Pakistan (1995), Annual Report – 1995, (www.sbp.org.pk), Karachi.

State Bank of Pakistan (1996), Annual Report – 1996, (www.sbp.org.pk), Karachi.

State Bank of Pakistan (1997), Annual Report – 1997, (www.sbp.org.pk), Karachi.

State Bank of Pakistan (1998), Annual Report – 1998, (www.sbp.org.pk), Karachi.

State Bank of Pakistan (1999), Annual Report – 1999, (www.sbp.org.pk), Karachi.

State Bank of Pakistan (2000), Annual Report – 2000, (www.sbp.org.pk), Karachi.

State Bank of Pakistan (2000), Pakistan Financial Sector Assessment (1990–2000), (www.sbp.org.pk), Karachi.

State Bank of Pakistan (2001), Annual Report – 2001, (www.sbp.org.pk), Karachi.

State Bank of Pakistan (2002), Annual Report – 2002, (www.sbp.org.pk), Karachi.

State Bank of Pakistan (2003), Annual Report – 2003, (www.sbp.org.pk), Karachi.

State Bank of Pakistan (2004), Annual Report – 2004, (www.sbp.org.pk), Karachi.

State Bank of Pakistan (2005), Annual Report – 2005, (www.sbp.org.pk), Karachi.

Suchman, M. C. (1995), 'Managing legitimacy: strategic and institutional approaches', *Academy of Management Journal*, Vol. 20 No. 3, pp. 571–610.

Sulaiman, S. and Mitchell, F. (2005), 'Utilising a typology of management accounting change: an empirical analysis', *Management Accounting Research*, Vol. 16, pp. 422–437.

Tangen, S. (2004), 'Performance measurement: from philosophy to practice', *International Journal of Productivity and Performance Management*, Vol. 53 No. 8, pp. 726–737.

The Asian Banker (2006), Vol 2, June – September 2006, Singapore, www.theasian banker.com.

The New York Times (2004), 'Global economies: a supplement published by Summit communications', September, 2004.

Tsamenyi, M., Cullen, J. and Gonzalez, J. M. G. (2006), 'Changes in accounting and financial information system in a Spanish electricity company: a new institutional theory analysis', *Management Accounting Research*, Vol. 17, pp. 409–432.

Uddin, S. and Hopper, T. (1999), 'Management control, ownership and development: experiences in privatised Bangladeshi enterprise', in Mackintosh, M. and Roy, R. (Eds), *Macro Reforms and Micro-processes: Political Economy and Economic Management*, London: Elgar.

Uddin, S. and Hopper, T. (2001), 'A Bangladesh soap opera: privatization, accounting, and regimes of control in a less developed country', *Accounting, Organizations and Society*, Vol. 26, pp. 643–672.

Uddin, S. and Tsamenyi, M. (2005), 'Public sector reforms and the public interest: a case research of performance monitoring in a Ghanaian State-Owned

Enterprise (SOE)', *Accounting Auditing and Accountability Journal*, Vol. 18 No. 5, pp. 648–675.

Vaivio, J. (1999), 'Exploring a 'non-financial' management accounting change', *Management Accounting Research*, Vol. 10, pp. 409–437.

Waggoner, D. B., Neely, A. D. and Kennerley, M. P. (1999), 'The forces that shape organizational performance measurement systems: an interdisciplinary review', *International Journal of Production Economics*, Vol. 60 No. 1, pp. 53–60.

Wagner, M., Stefan, S. and Walter, W. (2001), 'The relationship between the environmental and economic performance of firms. What does theory propose and what does empirical evidence tell us?', *Greener Management International*, Vol. 34, pp. 95–108.

Wallace, R. S. O. (1990), 'Accounting in developing countries', *Research in Third World Accounting*, Vol. 1, pp. 3–54.

Wanna, J., Jensen, L. and de Vries, J. (2003), *Controlling Public Expenditure*, UK: Edward Elgar Publishers.

Waterhouse, J. H. and Tiessen, P. (1978), 'A contingency framework for management accounting systems research', *Accounting, Organizations and Society*, Vol. 1, pp. 65–76.

Waweru, N. M., Hoque, Z. and Uliana, E. (2004), 'Management accounting change in South Africa: case studies from retail services', *Accounting, Auditing and Accountability Journal*, Vol. 17 No. 5, pp. 675–704.

Wickramasinghe, D. and Hopper, T. (2005), 'A cultural political economy of management accounting controls: a case research of a textile mill in a traditional Sinhalese village', *Critical Perspectives on Accounting*, Vol. 16 No. 4, pp. 473–503.

Wickramasinghe, D., Hopper, T. and Ratnasiri, C. (2004), 'Japanese cost management meets Sri Lankan politics: disappearance and reappearance of bureaucratic controls in a privatised utility', *Accounting, Auditing and Accountability Journal*, Vol. 17 No. 1, pp. 85–120.

Wignall, R. B. and Atkinson, P. (2010), 'Thinking beyond Basel III: necessary solutions for capital and liquidity', *OECD Journal: Financial Market Trends*, Vol. 2010 No. 1, pp. 1–23.

Williams, J. J. and Seaman, A. E. (2002), 'Management accounting systems change and departmental performance: the influence of managerial information and task uncertainty', *Management Accounting Research*, Vol. 13 No. 4, pp. 419–445.

World Bank (2000), '*Financial Sector update, Washington D.C., May 31, 2000*' cited in '*Reforms of Public Sector Banks – Case Research of Pakistan*', presented by the Governor State Bank of Pakistan at the World Bank Conference on Transforming Public Sector Banks, World Bank, Washington DC.

World Bank (2005), Annual Report – 2005, Office of Publisher, External Affairs (www. worldbank.org), Washington, DC.

World Bank (2006), Annual Report – 2006, Office of Publisher, External Affairs (www. worldbank.org), Washington, DC.

World Bank (2008), Annual Report – 2008, Office of Publisher, External Affairs (www. worldbank.org), Washington, DC.

World Bank (2009), Annual Report – 2009, Office of Publisher, External Affairs (www. worldbank.org), Washington, DC.

World Bank (2010), Annual Report – 2010, Office of Publisher, External Affairs (www. worldbank.org), Washington, DC.

Yazdifar, H., Zaman, M., Tsamenyi, M. and Askarany, D. (2008), 'Management accounting change in a subsidiary organisation', *Critical Perspective of Accounting*, Vol. 19, pp. 404–430.

Yin, R. K. (1993), *Applications of Case Research*, Beverly Hills, CA: SAGE.

Yin, R. K. (1994), *Case Research: Design and Methods*, Thousand Oaks, CA: SAGE.

Yin, R. K. (2001), *Case Research: Design and Methods*, Thousand Oaks, CA: SAGE.

Yin, R. K. (2002), *Case Research: Design and Methods*, Newbury Park, CA: SAGE.

Yin, R. K. (2003), *Case Research: Design and Methods*, Thousand Oaks, CA: Sage.

Young, S. M. and Selto, F. (1993), 'Explaining cross-sectional workgroup performance differences in a JIT facility: a critical appraisal of a field-based research', *Journal of Management Accounting Research*, Vol. 5, pp. 300–326.

Ziadi, I. M. (2005), '*Exchange rate flexibility and the monetary policy framework in Pakistan*', Presented at the SBP Conference on Monetary-cum-Exchange Rate: What Works Best for the Emerging Market Economies? State Bank of Pakistan, Karachi, November (www.sbp.org.pk).

Zimmerman, J. L. (2009), *Accounting for Decision Making and Control*, 6th edition, New York: McGraw-Hill Irwin.

Index

Note: Page numbers in *italics* indicate figures; those in **bold** indicate tables.